THE
SOUTHERN
GARDEN

Approximate Range of Average
Annual Minimum Temperatures
for Each Zone

Zone 6   5° to   5°
Zone 7   5° to 10°
Zone 8 10° to 20°
Zone 9 20° to 30°

THE SOUTHERN GARDEN

FROM THE POTOMAC
TO THE RIO GRANDE

BY BEN ARTHUR DAVIS

J. B. LIPPINCOTT COMPANY
PHILADELPHIA & NEW YORK

Introduction

In my two-year tenure as president of the National Council of State Garden Clubs I had occasion to visit more than half of the states in the Union, and on these travels I made it a point to observe the different horticultural practices in the various sections of the country. I observed at first hand how gardening is related to geography and climate. There may be a certain relation between gardening practices in New England and the Midwest, or in some areas of the Southwest and the Pacific Northwest, but there is no close relation between any of these various sections and our Southland.

The area south of the Ohio River, lying roughly between the Potomac and Rio Grande, is a garden region of its very own, and one cannot easily adapt to that area practices followed in any other section of the country.

Not only do climatic differences bring about a change in varieties and species, but also the time of planting of several large groups of plants is different, if not entirely reversed. To garden successfully in the South, one has to acquaint himself with the geography and climate of that region and also with the species which can and cannot be grown there.

I know of no person better qualified to write a book on gardening in the South than the author of *The Southern Garden*.

Mr. Davis has been connected with agriculture, horticulture and floriculture all of his life. He has lived close to the soil. For years he judged flower shows all the way from west Texas to the Atlantic seaboard; for more than twenty years he was a test grower for America's largest rose producer and at that time had a test garden of more than one hundred varieties of roses. He is without doubt the most prolific writer of garden literature in the South, having been garden editor for about twenty-five years of a magazine of more than five hundred thousand circulation and regional editor for several specialty horticulture societies. He has written four successful garden books prior to this one. For his contribution to the garden club movement he was awarded the silver medal by the National Council of State Garden Clubs three years ago.

The information contained within these pages was written by a Southern gardener thoroughly familiar with gardening conditions and well versed in the plant life of the entire South. He is recognized by successful gardeners as an authority on the subject. The subject matter has been presented in an easy-to-read manner.

The author expresses a desire to share his years of experience with fellow gardeners of the South; consequently, the reader will receive a spiritual warmth from these pages.

May the users of this excellent book find a happy and rewarding day in their gardens.

GERALDINE DEAN
(MRS. CHARLES O. DEAN)
Chairman, Advisory Board, and Past President
National Council of State Garden Clubs, Incorporated

Foreword

Having spent my childhood and early youth on the small farm and cattle and sheep ranch where I was born in South Mississippi, I developed early a love for all plant and animal life. The family owned or controlled several hundred acres of woodland in addition to the farm. Much of my time and that of my brothers was spent in the forest.

At an early age we learned to identify practically all the flora of the region by observing the foliage, and became familiar with practically every genus and species native to a radius of several miles.

When circumstances of economy required me to live in the city, it was but natural that I seek an outlet for my interest in plant life. Of course, it was necessary to reduce the scope of my activities materially and confine them to the dimensions of a city lot rather than a boundless forest.

I began looking for books on flower growing. This was the period of transition from the one-horse plow to modern farm machinery. Agricultural high schools were springing up all over the country, and the Extension Service was spreading its activities at a rapid rate. But I found few books or other literature on beautification, landscape design or growing flowers, and those few were written for use in the East or Midwest. The authors seemed to have overlooked the fact that there was also a large area south of the Ohio River, as well as a great Southwest, that was inhabited. The books available ignored this large area and could not be used in the Middle or Deep South.

I set about in search of books with a Southern application but was able to find only one, and it was soon withdrawn by the publisher because it contained too many errors and too much misinformation.

In the meantime a few books appeared that could be of some help to people trying to garden in the South, if they had a vivid imagination; but most of the information of successful gardeners in the South was gleaned from that old method of trial and error.

About thirty years ago, my *Holland's Handbook for Southern Gardeners* appeared on the market and met with a rather warm reception. But it is now somewhat outdated, and I have felt for several years that a new garden book for the South was in order.

In *The Southern Garden* I have tried to give you the best that could be developed for the busy Southerner, especially for those who need information and have a minimum of time to search for it.

The first half of the book, Section 1, is devoted to a kind of garden calendar, with several pages given to what to do each month in the Southern garden. I hope this will prove particularly valuable to gardeners who habitually overlook doing things when they should be done. By reading the suggestions for the month at hand, one should be able to get a grasp on the principal garden activities for that particular month. This section should be of special interest to our many friends from the colder areas who have moved to the South in recent years.

In Section 2 I have devoted chapters to subjects which I consider of special importance to gardeners in the Southern area. These are subjects which I think will appeal to practically every owner of home grounds in the South.

The subject of pruning ornamentals is of major importance, and while I did not devote an entire chapter to it I hope the reader will find answers to all his pruning questions in the chapter on Ornamental Shrubs

In Potpourri, I tried to give a bit of essential information on several subjects, space for which could not be found for full development in the main body of the book.

Gardeningly yours,
BEN ARTHUR DAVIS

Acknowledgments

To the members of the garden clubs throughout the South and Southwest who have worked so earnestly and so diligently these many years, not only to conserve and protect the natural beauty of our regions but to enhance it as well,

To my good Woman Friday, Sarah Combs Davis, who has been such a wonderful help in the closing days of the preparation of this manuscript,

To my good friend, Daisy C. Ellison, whose assistance in typing and editing has made this book possible and without whose able assistance it could never have gone to press,

And to my friend, Mildred Black, who assisted in typing the manuscript, I wish to express my appreciation.

I also wish to thank Arthur I. Coyle, Houston, Texas, for his valuable comments on the culture of rhododendrons; the U.S. Department of Agriculture for the cuts used in illustrations; and the University of Florida Extension Service for information contained in their bulletins.

Contents

Contents

Section 1

What to Do in the Garden:
A Monthly Calendar

1

January

In many sections of the South, January is a wet, cold, disagreeable month. There is less activity in the garden, perhaps, than during any other month of the year. Yet there are many things that can and should be done.

OUTDOOR TASKS

In many cases you will have to pick favorable days, but this is a good time to give the flower and shrub beds a general cleaning up. By removing old mulches and spent flowers from areas known to be infested with insects and diseases, and by surface spraying with a good insecticide-fungicide preparation, you will avoid many potential problems. You will get the bugs in all stages of development—hibernating insects, eggs and larvae—and destroy many fungi that could cause no end of trouble later in the season.

If sprays are applied when plants are dormant, much stronger solutions may be used than in sprays applied in summer when the leaves are tender. Roses, dogwoods, flowering almonds, peaches, lilacs, plums and cherries usually benefit from a dormant spray. Apply when the temperature is well above freezing.

3

Your garden store probably has the prepared sprays already mixed and ready for use.

All mulches should be checked this month. Three or four inches of straw do wonders in protecting azaleas, gardenias, camellias and other shrubs and young trees, and it is also important that young plants be kept well mulched. What about your amaryllis seedlings and other tender things? Have you given them sufficient protection to prevent freezing? In the Middle South, give mature amaryllis bulbs left in the ground a good mulch of straw.

Do not be in a hurry to do the winter pruning; next month will be time enough. Early pruning stimulates new growth which will, except in the Lower South (Zones 9 and 10), probably be killed by later freezes. However, you may shape up the evergreens now. Do not shear, but clip back branches here and there to induce thickening and the development of a better-shaped plant. Try to leave the specimen looking natural, as though it had not been touched by the shears. And by all means give injured trees and shrubs immediate attention: remove damaged branches and paint the wounds. In the Upper South (Zone 7), relatively heavy snows are to be expected, and we sometimes have them in Zone 8, the Middle South. (See map for zone areas.) If they come, be sure to remove the accumulation from the branches of your young pines and other evergreens to prevent damage from breaking.

Check azaleas after each hard freeze to see whether the bark has split on any of the canes. If so, bind them with ordinary mending tape and the wounds will soon heal; otherwise, the canes will gradually die out during the coming spring and summer.

While November and December are the best months to take most hardwood or winter cuttings, January is not too late for many species. If taken early this month, many cuttings of deciduous species will have time to root before hot weather gets here. But I would not wait longer for this work.

This is a good season for checking the design of the garden. Perhaps you may wish to change the size or shape of some of the beds, put in or take out a path or walk, or plant additional backgrounds. Annuals and perennials in most areas will have spent themselves by January, the deciduous shrubs are bare, and we can tell better where changes should be made. Let's look around and see if there are not some spots where another shrub, evergreen or clump of perennials should be added. Maybe we need another small tree. Or there may be some areas where things are beginning to get badly crowded and from which something should be moved in order to give room for better development of choice plants. Most of our plantings become a bit crowded as they grow older and will need some thinning here and there.

Remember the birds. Even in the Middle South (Zone 8), where the winters are comparatively mild, many species of birds have difficulty in finding sufficient food during our severe winter weather, especially in periods of heavy snow or sleet. Bread crumbs, suet and "wild-bird" grain mixture will save the lives of many birds and bring them to your grounds as daily winter visitors. While some are migratory, many of them will nest on your grounds if necessary vines, shrubs and trees are available.

You may get attractive bird feeders at the stores, or with little effort you can make them yourself. If there is a Boy Scout in the neighborhood, he will probably be happy to build attractive feeders for you. If nothing else is available, old bread pans or even pie tins, punched for drainage and tacked to the tops of posts, will help carry the birds through emergencies. Be sure to place the feeders out of reach of prowling cats. After you once begin to feed the birds, food should be placed for them daily until spring arrives, when they should be able to find an ample supply of insects to meet their needs.

Fish use little food in winter, but if ice forms over their pools for more than a day or two, break it to give them air.

INDOOR TASKS

Midwinter is an excellent time to repair the fences, garden fixtures and lawn furniture. In the workshop, make up a supply of labels and stakes for the chrysanthemums, gladioli, peonies and other plants that will require staking later in the season. Have the lawn mowers repaired if necessary. Clean and sharpen the tools; paint their handles a bright color so they will be easily found if lost. Although it may be chilly today, spring is just over the hill. Get all these winter jobs behind you and have more time for planting and transplanting when the warm days arrive.

Stored bulbs should be checked. If any appear too moist, place them in the sun for a day or two to dry out a bit; if, on the other hand, they seem to be a bit too dry and are shriveling, you had better sprinkle them with water. Caladium corms should be kept at a temperature of about 70 to 75 degrees all through the winter. If they get too cold they will rot, even though they do not freeze.

Every gardener should keep a garden scrapbook. If you have not already started one, January is a good month to get to it. Devote a section to each class of plants. Record all important garden events: source and cost of rare seeds and those of new varieties, bulbs and plants. Enter the time of planting, time of germination, when first blooms open, when peak of bloom was reached, date of last frost in spring and earliest one in fall. Make entries showing how basic plants withstood dry periods and which were damaged most by freezes. All this information will be helpful in planning and planting for the following season, and it may come in handy when you are called on to make a talk to your garden club.

GIFT PLANTS

If you received a living **Christmas tree** during the recent holidays, get it out into the ground at once. Water well after planting, even though the earth is fully moist. These living Christmas trees will go on for generations, giving greater beauty to the grounds each year and standing as a constant reminder of the thoughtfulness of the giver.

When the leaves turn yellow and the flowers fade on the potted **poinsettias**, place them in a dark corner of the garage, basement or other place where they will not freeze. Water only about once a month until spring, when they should be pruned back severely and repotted in fresh soil or planted outdoors in a partially shaded area. The prunings made when the plants are cut back are easily rooted if the wood is cut into lengths of about six inches and handled like other hardwood cuttings, but, of course, they should not be permitted to freeze.

Hardy bulbs should be planted outdoors just as soon as the flowers have faded; don't allow these plants to dry up and die.

When the blooms of forced **chrysanthemums** have faded, prune very low, discard the tops and either unpot and set the plants in the garden beds or set the pots in a protected area. If you have a greenhouse, this would be an ideal place for storing the pots until spring. These plants, properly sprayed, fed and watered now, should give you many good cuttings in just a few weeks.

HOUSE PLANTS

January is a very difficult month for most house plants. The use of artificial heat is at its height, and the temperature in our houses is usually high and the air quite dry. Overheated rooms and lack of moisture spell the doom of many plants.

Keep **African violets and cyclamens** in a moderately cool room, and water them by placing the containers in a pan of water for several hours at twice-a-week intervals; never water these plants from the top.

The lack of proper sunlight usually results in some straggly, leggy growth among indoor plants, especially in the window gardens where we are inclined to crowd the plants. Removing this excessive growth will add much to the beauty of the plants by inducing a more shapely development.

To lengthen the stems of forced **hyacinths,** roll a sheet of paper into a cylinder, secure with a rubber band and slip down over the stem when it is about an inch long. A flower pot inverted over the plant will give approximately the same results. Remove the covering when the stem has attained the proper length.

Fuchsias may be started into growth this month, and **gloxinias**

may be potted, using plenty of sand in the soil. **Lilies-of-the-valley** should bloom in four or five weeks from pips if given a temperature of 75 to 80 degrees.

WHAT TO PLANT

You may still plant daffodils and other **spring-flowering bulbs** (except tulips), if they are in sound, firm condition. You may even plant tulips if they have been precooled for several weeks. Many stores offer these bulbs at greatly reduced prices this month. You may find some of them worthless, but if they are still firm they should be all right. Many bulbs only slightly soft will firm up if soaked in water for twenty-four hours; those that do not plump up with this treatment are not worth planting. Of course, bulbs planted in January will be a bit late in blooming.

Continue planting **bare-root roses, shrubs, and trees;** also **balled and burlapped evergreens** of all kinds. We have a long planting season in the South for shrubby things, but we must not put off planting till too late. Midwinter is the best time to plant most of these items. In our moderately warm Southern climate, roots of shrubs hardly stop growing all winter and the shrubs begin making new roots right after being planted. If we plant them in December or January, they will have time to become established and make considerable root growth before spring arrives.

In selecting trees for the home grounds, we should consider their ultimate height, character of growth and root system. If we are not familiar with these characteristics, we should inquire of the seller; if he does not know, we had better not take a chance. Be sure that every tree and shrub chosen meets the special requirements of the particular spot in which it is to be placed. The most common mistake is to plant trees where shrubs are appropriate.

It is usually difficult to grow grass and flowers under such shallow-rooted trees as maples and elms. Deep-rooted kinds, like red oaks, white oaks and the nut trees, give much less trouble and should usually be selected. But in planting flowers and grass under trees of any type it is well to keep in mind that liberal portions of both food and moisture must be supplied. The trees usually get theirs in any event, and the flowers and grass come in for a much smaller share.

Unless it has been treated with a preservative, the burlap need not be removed from balled and burlapped plants when planting, but be careful not to break the ball. Balled plants should never be lifted from the trunk or top; always place one hand under the ball. The burlap may be loosened at the top and rolled back so you can see how deep to set the plant. The top of the ball should be approximately at ground level.

Canned plants, as a rule, should be removed from the can with the earth intact. Where these plants are grown in ordinary tin cans, the same size at top and bottom, it is usually better to have the nurseryman slit the cans with tin shears so the plants can be readily removed from the container with the earth intact. Of course, if you have the proper tools you can do the slitting yourself.

January and February are very good months for planting all kinds of **fruit trees** in the South. In the Lower South (Zone 9), complete the planting this month; farther north, by the middle of February. When planting, stake all trees an inch or more in diameter as a protection from wind, animals and children. Use a soft cord to tie the tree to the stake, if possible. If you must use wire, wrap it so that it will not cut the bark of the tree.

Azaleas and camellias may be planted now also; you do not have to wait until they are in bloom. Although both genera may be easily handled when in bloom, and that is the time when most of them are planted, it is definitely not the best time to plant. Like roses and other shrubby things, they will go into their first season with a much better root system if planted early. However, if you do not know what you want in azaleas and camellias, you had better wait and see the plants in bloom before buying. (If you live in the "camellia belt," try to attend at least one good camellia show each season, to make selections of varieties you will wish to plant and to see a maximum number of the new and unusual varieties.)

Bulbous items you may plant this month include alstroemeria, anemone, billbergia, butterfly lily, ginger lily, liriope and oxalis. (See fuller planting list below.)

In Zones 9 and 10, the Rio Grande Valley, along the Gulf Coast, and in Florida, you may plant seeds of **hardy annuals** early this month and continue right on through the winter. But in Zones 7 and 8, Upper and Middle South, not much if anything can be gained by planting seed this month, unless you have a greenhouse where moisture and temperature can be controlled; in this area let's wait until February or March. If you will get seeds of the hardy annuals in November or December, or even in early January, and precool them in the refrigerator several weeks before planting, the germination should be much better and the seedlings will get a better start.

You may also plant many **vegetables** now in Zones 9 and 10, especially the "greens." Try lettuce, English peas, tendergreens, turnips, beets, carrots, Chinese cabbage and collards. Even though there are a few failures, the chances of success make the effort entirely worthwhile. In more northern areas there is little you can do in the vegetable garden this month.

PLANTING LIST FOR JANUARY

Seeds

Alyssum
Anchusa
*Arctotis
*Calendula
Calliopsis
*Candytuft (Iberis)
Cleome
*Coreopsis,
  perennial

Cornflower
  (Centaurea)
Gaillardia
Larkspur
Lobelia
Lupine
*Pentstemon
Petunia
Phlox, annual

Poppy, annual
Queen Anne's lace
*Snapdragon
  (Antirrhinum)
Stock
Sweet pea
Verbena
Wallflower
  (Cheiranthus)

Bulbs, Rhizomes and Tubers

Allium
Alstroemeria
Amaryllis
Anemone
Billbergia
Butterfly lily
  (Hedychium)
Calla lily
  (Zantedeschia)
Camassia
Clivia
Daffodil
  (Narcissus)

Freesia
Ginger lily
  (Zingiber)
Gladiolus
Grape hyacinth
  (Muscari)
Hyacinth
Leucocoryne
Liatris
Liriope
Ornithogalum
Oxalis

Ranunculus
Red-hot poker
  (Kniphofia)
Scilla
Snowdrop
  (Galanthus)
Snowflake
  (Leucojum)
Tulip
Wandflower
  (Sparaxis)

---

* Plant in protected beds.

2

February

Although February, like January, is many times a very severe winter month, we know that spring cannot be very far away. There are many garden chores that must be gotten out of the way before warm weather arrives. In order to get all these things attended to in time, let's get busy right away.

WHAT TO PLANT

I do not know how it is with others, but we are rarely ever able to get all our **hardy annuals** planted in the fall. If you did not plant earlier, you may now plant seeds of alyssum, calendula, California and annual poppies, calliopsis, clarkia, cleome, corn-flower, larkspur and phlox; and, although I think fall planting is better, there are many gardeners who traditionally plant sweet peas on or about St. Valentine's Day. In Florida, the Rio Grande Valley and the Deep South (Zones 9 and 10), you may begin planting these hardy annuals early in the month; in the Upper South (Zone 7), late in the month.

Seeds of **biennials** should normally be planted in summer or early fall so that one will have strong plants for setting out in November. However, if you can find strong, choice plants at the nursery stores, you may plant them this month. But keep in mind that young, weak biennial plants set out now will probably not bloom the coming season. If you set out plants this month, be sure to get strong ones.

There have been tremendous improvements in foxgloves and hollyhocks in recent years. Of course, it is too late to plant seeds but you may run across strong plants at the garden stores. Tiny seedlings may not bloom this season, but strong plants should bloom well. You'll love them.

As for **bulbs, tubers and rhizomes,** toward the last of the month you may plant acidanthera, agapanthus, amaryllis, crinum, gladiolus, hosta, montbretia, red-hot poker, tigridia and zephyranthes in the Middle South (Zone 8).

Caladiums are hot-weather plants, but if you have a greenhouse, heated garage or sunny window you may start the corms indoors this month and be weeks ahead of the outdoor plantings.

In many sections of the South, February is a good time to make a first planting of **gladiolus.** Early planting usually gives the best flowers, as they bloom before hot, dry weather arrives. Most gardeners make several plantings of gladiolus, spaced a few weeks apart, in order to have continuous bloom.

Thrips are the greatest enemies of gladiolus, and while most good nurseries treat the corms before shipping, the safe thing is to treat them yourself before planting, as the thrip lives over the winter in the corm. Place the corms in paper bags and add two tablespoonfuls of naphthalene flakes (moth flakes) for each hundred corms, roll the top of the bag down to prevent the escape of fumes, shake and let stand at least two weeks before planting. Soaking them for three or four hours in a solution of Lysol, a tablespoonful to a gallon of water, is also usually very effective.

While **watsonias** are a bit more tender than gladiolus, both genera will stand quite a bit of cold and may be planted in the Middle South (Zone 8) during the last half of the month. Although not so well known in the South, watsonias are very pretty and are easily grown. In many respects they are very much like the gladiolus, but their blooming season is longer. Adelaide (pink), Lucille (salmon), Malvern (orchid) and Mrs. Ballard's White are varieties you will like.

The **daffodils** are glorious now in most sections of the South. This is a good time to select clumps to be grouped or divided, or to note where additional plantings should be made. Do not disturb the bulbs in any way until the foliage has matured.

In the Deep South many **perennials** will begin growing late in the month. When this new growth is two to four inches high, the clumps may be divided and replanted, if that is to be done this season. Hardy asters, physostegia, phlox and Shasta-type daisies begin growing early and should be divided before strong growth develops. If you have clumps of daylilies that are to be divided this spring, get to them just as soon as the new growth is a few inches high. (For chrysanthemums, see Chapter 16.)

While you probably made a planting of Dutch iris last fall, you may make another planting late this month if you like. Few flowers surpass these for cutting, and they work well into most all kinds of arrangements.

Throughout most sections of the South this is the last call for planting **bare-root shrubs, trees and roses.** It will add interest to our plantings if we introduce at least one new shrub each season. Get something that will fit into the planting, of course, but let it be a species or variety that is somewhat new. A search of the catalogs or a visit to a nearby nursery will usually reveal something unusual.

This is a good month for planting both azaleas and camellias. By visiting nurseries and sales yards now you will be able to see many of them in bloom and be able to make proper selections. In planning your planting, don't overlook the possibilities of the white azaleas. They possess an independent beauty and are invaluable for separating colors, such as the varying reds which might otherwise clash. Reeves' spirea (*Spiraea reevesiana*) is another good white choice for planting between clumps of azaleas of different colors. It makes a lovely mass and usually comes into bloom with the midseason azaleas.

The **Japanese quince,** *Chaenomeles japonica,* may now be had in several colors: salmon, pink, rose, red and white. In many sections of the South it is now in bloom and is almost as showy as the azaleas. Branches may easily be forced by being placed in vases of water in a sunny window. This is an old but very valuable shrub. It is especially showy when in full bloom in January and February before the leaves appear. Some varieties continue blooming well into the spring.

If you wish rank growth, a solid background, fruit for the birds and winter flowers that will give a winelike fragrance that will cause everyone to stop and wonder, all from one shrub, then plant the **Elaeagnus.** A freeze will kill the flowers and buds, but on our plants there are plenty more within three or four days after the weather turns warm again. It blooms right on for two or three months—and what a fragrance!

February is a busy month in **the vegetable garden** throughout the entire South. Across the northern section of Mississippi, Alabama, Georgia and to the east, plant English peas, cabbage, collards, onions, spinach and lettuce. To the south you can plant beets, carrots, Chinese cabbage, endive, kohlrabi, lettuce, mustard, radishes, turnips, spinach, rutabagas, English peas and potatoes late in the month. An early planting is desirable even if a late frost does sometimes catch a few of the seedlings.

Those Christmas cyclamens may soon stop blooming and give evidence of wanting a rest. If so, store them in a cool room until spring, then plunge the pot in soil in a shady spot, watering occasionally during the summer. If the plant survives, growth will start in the fall, when the plant should be repotted in good soil.

PRUNING

The secret of timing the winter pruning is to do it immediately after the last severe cold spell, but since this date cannot be determined precisely, we must take a chance. If pruned too early, many plants will be stimulated to premature growth that will be killed by later cold. Pruned too late, the plants will not have time to make proper growth.

Prune bush roses, crape myrtle, althea, vitex and other **summer-flowering shrubs.** (Do not prune shrubs that flower in the spring such as spirea, forsythia, deutzia, pearlbush and weigela.) In the Lower South (Zone 9), do this winter pruning about the middle of the month; in the Middle South (Zone 8), around Washington's Birthday; and in the Upper South (Zone 7), about the last of the month.

In pruning, check the plants carefully for badly diseased twigs and branches, winter-killed twigs and those that have been otherwise badly damaged. Remove all of these, cutting back to sound wood.

Practically all **shade and ornamental trees** may be pruned this month. In cutting off large branches, make the first saw cut underneath, about fifteen or twenty inches from the main trunk; then cut from the top; last, remove the stub flush with the trunk.

In pruning **hedges** do not make the common error of leaving them broader at the top than near the ground. A hedge should be a few inches broader at the ground than at the top, to enable the sunlight to reach all surfaces and prevent twigs and foliage from drying out near the ground.

There is a bit of controversy over the extent to which **established roses** should be pruned in the South, but many tests have indicated that there is danger in overpruning. Lightly pruned bush roses will normally give many more flowers, so do not take off more than one third to one half of the wood, removing, of course, all blind canes and twigs.

If you have wisterias, bougainvilleas or other **vines** that have not been blooming properly, try root pruning. This is done by inserting a spade several inches deep in a circle about fifteen or eighteen inches from the trunk of the plant; if the plant is small, make a circle proportionately smaller.

FEEDING

When the first leaf buds begin to swell, it is time to feed your roses, shrubs and trees. With root feeders you should be able to get food to the roots, where it will be available at once.

In most cases where trees appear stunted, sick and lacking in vigor, they are merely being starved to death. Feed your trees this month if you want them to be vigorous and healthy. Use any good commercial plant food. If the tree is quite small, just dig the food into the soil under its branches. But if it is as much as four inches in diameter, do not make the mistake of placing the plant food near the trunk; get it out under the drips of the branches so that it will be available to the thousands of tiny feed roots. The best plan is to dig holes, two or three feet apart and a foot deep, in a circle under the ends of the branches; then mix 6-8-8 or similar fertilizer with soil, fill the holes and replace the sod. For large trees you may have to dig two or three circles of holes in order to give them adequate food. From one half to one pound of plant food for each inch of circumference, measured four feet above the ground, should give good results, but half this amount will be of great help to starved trees.

This is a good time to feed the **climbing roses,** that group of plants so frequently overlooked. For old established plants, use two or three heaping tablespoonfuls of balanced plant food, lightly dug in and well watered down. For young plants one or two tablespoonfuls would probably be sufficient. This is the time for feeding the bush roses and shrubs also. About three pounds of plant food, analyzing about 6-8-8, per hundred square feet of bed is the usual application for roses. Where plants are grown in beds, scatter the food over the bed, rake lightly in and water.

Feed your **daffodils** just after the new leaves peep through the surface of the ground. Around each clump dig in a mixed handful of bone meal and a complete garden fertilizer.

Do *not* feed azaleas and camellias this month. Wait until the flowers have faded from each particular species.

Pansies should be in full bloom now. Keep the faded flowers picked clean, give the plants a feeding of liquid fertilizer every two weeks (use as directed), and see that they get plenty of water. With this treatment they should bloom late into the spring.

In the Rio Grande Valley and through central and southern Florida, where the **annuals** are in full bloom, the faded flowers should be clipped and the plants given a light feeding of good balanced plant food (6-8-8), about two pounds to each hundred square feet of bed, or a like amount for each hundred feet of row. For such flowers as English daisies and pansies I prefer liquid fertilizer, but be sure to use it according to directions. If any fertilizer falls on the foliage or stems, wash it off with the garden hose.

From Houston to New Orleans, Pensacola and across Florida this is an excellent month to repair and remake old lawns and establish new ones. Do not expect grass to thrive in soils where other plant life cannot flourish. For a good sod you must have at least a few inches of good soil on the surface. Feed your lawn this month regardless of whether you planted rye grass or not.

PLANT PROPAGATION

It is getting a bit late in the season for taking hardwood cuttings, but you may take cuttings of most ornamental species early this month with a moderate degree of success. Taken this late, the cuttings should be placed in a bed where they can remain undisturbed until next fall.

While this is not the ideal time to take evergreen cuttings, if taken now many will root by late spring. Cover them either by turning jars over them or placing them in a covered frame.

Examine plants layered in the summer and fall. If well rooted, sever the branch between the roots and the mother plant and handle as a new specimen.

CONTROL OF PESTS AND DISEASE

Many insects live through our warm winters; this is especially true of the several species of aphids. The daylilies and chrysanthemums should be checked late this month or early in March—you will probably find aphids present. If so, spray with a good contact insecticide, forcing the spray right down into the crowns of the plants.

Watch the young tulips now for green aphids, which will do

untold damage if not checked. Any good contact insecticide should check them, but two or three applications may be necessary. Apply it at weekly intervals.

Along the Gulf Coast and from central Florida southward, many of the annuals should be in fine bloom this month. Watch the sweet peas for **red spiders**, and, if found, spray with insecticide. These and other annuals may be fed with the liquid mixture suggested for pansies. Keep all fading flowers clipped.

This is a good time to spray lawns for control of **wild garlic and onions**. Then wait two or three weeks. If you fail to get a "kill," repeat the application. Or you may find a special killer at the garden stores.

Azalea petal blight can be controlled by the use of a dependable spray, but it must be used persistently in order to get results. Follow the manufacturer's directions carefully.

There is still time to apply a dormant oil spray to peaches, almonds, lilacs and other plants susceptible to **scale**, provided the leaf buds are not developing. If the leaf buds show growth, better wait until later and use a summer-strength spray.

Pill bugs and cutworms will be troublesome this month and next. Just tell your seedsman or garden center man what pest you want to get rid of, and he'll be able to suggest a good remedy. The important point is to use it as directed.

PLANTING LIST FOR FEBRUARY

Seeds

*Ageratum
Alyssum
*Amaranthus
Anchusa
Arctotis
*Aster
*Baby blue-eyes
   (Nemophila)
Baby's-breath
   (Gypsophila)
*Blue laceflower
   (Trachymene or
   Didiscus)
Calendula
Calliopsis
Candytuft (Iberis)
Canterbury bells

Carnation
   (Dianthus)
Chinese
   forget-me-not
   (Cynoglossum)
*Clarkia
Cleome
*Cockscomb
   (Celosia)
Coreopsis, perennial
Cornflower
   (Centaurea)
Dimorphotheca
Feverfew
*Foxglove
Gaillardia
*Godetia
Lantana

Larkspur
Linaria
Lobelia
Lupine
Mallow (Malva)
Nasturtium
*Nicotiana
Nierembergia
Pentstemon
Petunia
Phlox, annual
Salpiglossis
*Salvia
Scabiosa
Sweet William
Verbena
Wallflower
   (Cheiranthus)

Bulbs, Rhizomes and Tubers

Achimenes
Acidanthera
Agapanthus
Allium
Amaryllis
Billbergia
Blackberry lily
   (Belamcanda)
Butterfly lily
   (Hedychium)
Calla lily
   (Zantedeschia)

Climbing lily
   (Gloriosa)
Clivia
Crinum
Daylily
   (Hemerocallis)
Ginger lily
   (Zingiber)
Gladiolus
Hosta
Iris, Dutch
Jacobaean lily
   (Sprekelia)

Liriope
Montbretia
Oxalis
Rain lily
   (Zephyranthes)
Red-hot poker
   (Kniphofia)
Scilla
Spider lily
   (Hymenocallis)
Tigridia

---

* Plant in protected beds.

3

March

March is a month of transition, from winter gardening to spring gardening. Although we may be having occasional cold snaps all through the month, and once in a while there may be ice and enough frost to kill tender things, there will also be some bright balmy days—days that will make the blood tingle and run warmer and the seeds sprout. We must hurry now to complete those jobs that should be finished before summer weather arrives.

WHAT TO PLANT

There is still time to plant some bare-root shrubs, roses and small trees before leaf buds begin to grow, if we dig and handle them carefully. Plants kept in cool storage, as many of the roses are being handled now, may be planted much later than material freshly dug from the nursery, because the low temperature prevents bud development.

Another very important factor in late planting is to see that plenty of water is used. After placing the plant, fill the hole half or two thirds full of soil, fill with water and, after this has soaked in, finish filling with earth. Unless ample rain falls, water the newly planted material well at least once each week.

21

Experience tells us that there are many things that may be moved successfully out of their normal season if carefully dug with earth at the roots. In handling out-of-season planting, we also find the rooting chemicals a great help.

If you are counting on planting more **fruit or shade trees**, you had better get this job finished as soon as possible: the roots need to be growing. Deciduous things planted bare-root in March should be more severely cut back than when planted in early winter.

Early March is a good time to plant both **dogwoods** and the **native Southern magnolias**, as growth begins at once and tends to check any "bleeding" from the roots that might develop.

This is the month when thousands of us will be planting **azaleas**. If you buy from the stores, do not accept plants that are wilted; take only the ones that are fresh and green. Plant immediately, water well and keep the plants shaded for a week or longer. Should rainfall be light, water these newly set plants twice each week, as they are shallow rooted and must have frequent watering.

Now is the time to take the **poinsettias** out of the basement, prune them back to within a few inches of the surface and repot. If the pots are plunged in soil in a shady spot outdoors until fall, they will be less trouble.

Around Shreveport, Vicksburg, Meridian and Montgomery, **tender annuals** like marigolds and zinnias may be planted in protected beds for later transplanting to the garden. A light covering will protect the seedlings from late frost. Handled in this way, the flowers should give bloom a week or two ahead of the usual flowering season.

By the last of the month in the Middle South (Zone 8), with a normal season, it should be safe to plant seeds of alyssum, amaranthus, anchusa, arctotis, cockscomb, marigold, periwinkle, petunia, portulaca, salvia, torenia and zinnia. Set out plants of marigold, petunia, plumbago, salvia, shrimp plant and torenia, if available.

Discounting the possibility of a late freeze, seeds of most annuals may now be planted outdoors in the Lower and Deep South (Zones 9 and 10). Use your own judgment and plant when you consider the danger of frost is past. To be perfectly safe, however, and to ensure getting an early start, I suggest planting most seeds in protected beds (where they may be covered if frost threatens) or, better still, in flats. Flats may be moved from place to place to take advantage of better sunlight and give proper protection from the elements. A heavy rain can prove disastrous to your seedlings unless they have protection of some kind.

Little volunteer plants in the old flower beds will make fine flowers if transplanted now. They are usually hardier, have better root systems and come into bloom earlier than plants from hand-sown seeds. Anyway, these little heroes who fought so valiantly for their lives during the winter should be given a chance to prove their worth.

The improved strain of amaranthus, *A. tricolor splendens,* is one of the most colorful foliage plants you will find anywhere. It stands dry weather well, and only a few plants will light up a huge flower bed, so gay are their colors. Give them plenty of sun for best color effects.

It is too late to plant seeds of **biennials**; also, it is too late to set out plants unless you can locate very strong ones. Weak plants set out now will probably not bloom this season.

Not all **perennials**, of course, should be separated and replanted each year, but when separation is done in the spring it should be done early. This gives the plants a longer period in which to make new roots and become established before the spring or summer blooming season. When clumps of perennials are not separated in the fall, it is a mistake to wait until there is lush growth in the spring, which is usually accompanied by hot weather.

Many of them may be handled in early March when the new growth is only two or three inches high. Check on those varieties making rapid new growth and give them first attention. When you are ready to divide the clumps, it is much better to dig the entire clump, wash or shake off the soil and divide with a sharp knife. By this method you should be able to see just where the division can best be made.

If the clumps of cannas failed to give good bloom last year, separate and replant them this month or early in April. Of course we have gotten away from planting large beds of cannas on the lawn, but clumps tucked back in the bays and coves of the shrub borders, where they have a good background, will add much color and beauty to the landscape.

Bulbous items which may be planted during the early part of the month in this area include achimenes, billbergia, blackberry lily, butterfly lily, climbing lily, clivia, crinum, dahlia, daylily, ginger lily, gladiolus, ismene, Jacobaean lily, liriope, montbretia, oxalis, and zephyranthes.

A little frost seems to do no damage to **gladiolus**, and I am convinced that, while the planting season for these flowers is a long one in the South, early planting gives best flowers. Let's make a planting early in the month, with additional plantings at two-week intervals until early summer.

Many of us in the South do not dig our **dahlias** for the winter. If they were left in the ground, they should be coming up now. If so, the clumps should be lifted with care, the earth washed off and the divisions made with a sharp knife. Leave a section of the old stem with each tuber. If the young eyes or sprouts are broken off, those particular tubers are worthless, as no more buds will grow.

Much of the success with dahlias, especially in producing mammoth exhibition blooms, depends on proper soil preparation and planting. Prepare the hole for each tuber as for a shrub or rose, digging it some twenty inches square, almost as deep, and refilling with prepared soil. Dahlias like a deep, rich soil and plenty of water, but the drainage should be satisfactory.

If you are adding **daylilies** this spring, get them planted at once, before hot weather arrives. They are among the easiest of all flowers to transplant, but while they are in lush growth is definitely not the best time to plant.

In the Middle South plant seeds of such **vegetables** as carrots, turnips, mustard, spinach, lettuce, and other semihardy species. Plants of tomatoes and peppers may also be set out. In the Deep South you may plant, in addition to the above, string beans, bunch beans, cucumbers, corn and melons.

PRUNING

Now let's consider the winter pruning, if that has not yet been done. Only roses and those species like crape myrtle, althea, summer-flowering spirea and vitex which bloom in summer should be pruned now. Spring-flowering shrubs must not be pruned until they have finished blooming, but get to them just as soon as the flowers fade.

Pillar roses and the everblooming climbers like Crimson Glory and Peace will need very little pruning, but the cluster types that send up long canes from the ground each spring should be pruned heavily right after the flowers fade. Cut the old canes off near the ground, or at least down to the first new cane. It is these new canes that give the flowers for the following spring.

FEEDING

Shrubs, roses, evergreens and trees should have been fed in February, but if you failed to do it then it is not too late to feed these things now.

Of course you fed your bush roses when you pruned them last month, but what of the climbers? Of all plants on our Southern home grounds, the **climbing roses** and perennial vines are probably the most neglected. Be sure to feed them this very week if you have not already attended to that chore.

The best time to feed **camellias** is right after the flowers have faded, which usually means March in most areas. If you use one of the special azalea-camellia plant foods you will hardly need to apply additional acid, but if you use standard garden fertilizer you'd better add some aluminum sulphate, iron sulphate or sulphur, or one of the newer iron chelates. I have found the chelates very good for restoring color to badly yellowed azaleas. If they are used, be careful to follow the instructions on the package.

Some gardeners say it is not necessary to keep faded flowers picked from **English daisies and pansies** in order to keep them in bloom, but if you remove all faded blooms, give regular applications of liquid food, and water if the weather is dry, you will definitely get a much longer flowering season. From nature's point of view the chief function of a plant is the formation of seed to propagate its kind. If we permit seeds to form, many will call it a season and fade out of the picture.

PLANT PROPAGATION

Cuttings of various shrubs, including **azaleas and camellias,** placed in the sand last summer and fall should be satisfactorily rooted now and can be moved to the growing beds. Using a large spoon, spatula or small trowel, lift carefully with a quantity of rooting sand with each cutting, handle carefully and replant without shaking off the sand. Water all cuttings well immediately after transplanting. Choose a shady spot in the growing bed for the azaleas and camellias.

This is the month for taking cuttings for new **chrysanthemum plants.** Feed the old clumps early in the month to encourage new growth. For new plants, take the tips of the new growth when it is three to three and a half inches high and root in a mixture of peat moss and sand. These early rooted cuttings will furnish stock plants from which additional cuttings may be taken a few weeks later if you need them. After you have all the cuttings you need, the old clumps should be discarded. The old woody roots of chrysanthemums are susceptible to attacks from termites—and termites can be disastrous.

Give your house plants a general renovation this month. No doubt there are some you will wish to discard and replace with new ones next fall, and you will want to take cuttings from others for the development of new plants. Still others should be placed outdoors as soon as danger of frost is past. In the case of house plants, it is usually the new tender growth that roots quickest and gives the best plants. Do not take large branches, just short pieces three to four inches long. Half coarse sand mixed with half peat moss gives a good rooting medium.

CONTROL OF PESTS AND DISEASE

This is the season when practically all **insects** feel the urge to increase the size of their families. When there is an abundance of youngsters present is the best time to apply insecticides. A moderately strong application will kill practically all forms of insect life when the bugs are young, but after they mature and develop protective coats much stronger solutions may be necessary (see Chapter 28). Most of these little rascals breed amazingly fast—a half dozen destroyed in March could mean having to destroy thousands less, later in the season.

Roses are now in nice growth, or soon will be, and you should begin the use of a dependable fungicide. Either dust or spray will do the job—just be sure you select a dependable one and apply it regularly, at weekly or ten-day intervals. What must you do if a rain washes off the fungicide? Make another application just as soon as you can, but definitely within twenty-four hours after the rain (see Chapter 28).

Azalea growers should begin spraying in order to prevent disastrous attacks of **bloom blight**. It will be too late after the flowers have all wilted.

Across the Upper South (Zone 7), March is a good time to dust or spray the bearded irises to check the **borers**.

PLANTING LIST FOR MARCH
Seeds

*Ageratum
Alyssum
*Amaranthus
Anchusa
Arctotis
*Aster
Baby blue-eyes
  (Nemophila)
Baby's-breath
  (Gypsophila)
Blue laceflower
  (Trachymene or
  Didiscus)
Calendula
Calliopsis
Candytuft (Iberis)
Canterbury bells
Chinese
  forget-me-not
  (Cynoglossum)

Clarkia
Cleome
Cockscomb
  (Celosia)
Coreopsis, perennial
Cornflower
  (Centaurea)
Dahlia
Dimorphotheca
Feverfew
Gaillardia
Godetia
Lantana
Larkspur
Linaria
Lobelia
Lupine
Mallow (Malva)
Marigold

Nasturtium
Nicotiana
Nierembergia
Pentstemon
Periwinkle
  (Vinca rosea)
Petunia
Phlox, annual
Platycodon
Portulaca
Salpiglossis
Salvia
Scabiosa
Stock
Torenia
Verbena
Wallflower
  (Cheiranthus)
Zinnia

Bulbs, Rhizomes and Tubers

Achimenes
Allium
Amaryllis
Billbergia
Blackberry lily
  (Belamcanda)
Butterfly lily
  (Hedychium)
Calla lily
  (Zantedeschia)
Climbing lily
  (Gloriosa)
Clivia

Crinum
Dahlia
Daylily
  (Hemerocallis)
Ginger lily
  (Zingiber)
Gladiolus
Gloxinia
Iris
  Japanese
  Louisiana
Ismene

Jacobaean lily
  (Sprekelia)
Liriope
Montbretia
Oxalis
Rain lily
  (Zephyranthes)
Red-hot poker
  (Kniphofia)
Spider lily
  (Hymenocallis)
Tigridia

* Plant in protected beds.

4

April

Spring is here! The sun is shining, the temperature is rising, the weeds are growing, the flowers are blooming and, last but not least, the insects are busy. All of us will find plenty to do on our home grounds this month.

WHAT TO PLANT

From Tyler, Shreveport and Atlanta to the coast we may transplant seedlings of **annuals** where danger of frost is behind us. Many gardeners let seedlings deteriorate from crowding in the beds. Be sure to lift them before this happens. If they once become leggy, they may never fully recover, although it may help to pinch out their buds. Even summer annuals may be planted in the open by the middle of the month. Let's hurriedly run through the list of good ones: ageratum, alyssum, amaranthus, anchusa, arctotis, baby's-breath, balsam, blue laceflower, cockscomb, cosmos, cleome, feverfew, gourds, linaria, nasturtium, periwinkle, portulaca, salvia and torenia.

It is too late to plant seeds of **biennials** for bloom this season, but not too late to set out good strong container-grown plants if you can find them at the garden stores. Container-grown bedding plants are usually cheaper in the long run. One year we needed some annuals in a hurry to prepare for convention visitors, so we bought two hundred bare-root petunias, some of which were almost in bloom. We lost all of them except five. A few years later we were caught in the same embarrassing situation but found some container-grown plants. Out of two hundred we did not lose a single plant. Container-grown plants will probably cost a little more, but they are well worth the difference.

If you have any more **perennials** that must be separated and replanted this spring, you had better do it right away before new growth gets any larger and before hot weather gets here. When considerable growth has already been made, it would probably be better to cut the plants back when they are separated. If practicable, pick a cloudy day for this work and use root-promoting chemicals.

If your cannas failed to bloom properly last season, perhaps they are crowded. If they are more than three years old, it would be wise to dig them up, separate and replant them in enriched soil. Some of the new cannas have immense blooms of rich, brilliant colors and make an impressive display for many months during summer. The dwarf types are very popular and are easily grown.

Much transplanting will be in order this month—annuals from the seedbeds and the stores, perennials, and a few late shrubs and roses that we did not get to earlier. The root-inducing hormones are a great help in transplanting everything from the tiniest seedlings to large shrubs and small trees. These chemicals greatly reduce the shock to plants and stimulate new root growth to start at once. You will not regret using them generously in your transplanting. In the absence of root hormones, always try to water recently transplanted things with a weak solution of liquid fertilizer.

Here's a lesson from the nurseryman: When it is necessary to handle small plants with roots which are completely bare, and which must stay out of the ground for more than a few hours, mix a little clay in a pail of water to the consistency of house paint and dip the roots into it. The clay retards the evaporation of moisture and reduces damage from exposure. But even with this treatment, roots should not be exposed any longer than absolutely necessary.

Although I do not recommend moving shrubby plants as late as April in the South, it sometimes becomes necessary to shift a few. In such cases, it can be done with a fair degree of success if they are dug with a ball of earth about the roots and planted immediately. Keep them well watered and shaded for a few weeks.

There is still time to plant such permanent vines as wisteria, climbing roses, clematis, Queen's wreath (*Antigonon leptopus*) and silver lace.

It is now warm enough to plant all kinds of **summer-flowering bulbous things**. Even the half-hardy ones may go into the ground by the middle of the month. Consider planting achimenes, allium, caladium, calla lily, canna, climbing lily, crinum, dahlia, daylily, gladiolus, hosta, ismene, liriope, montbretia, red-hot poker, spider lily, tigridia, tuberose and watsonia.

Hosta loves a shady, fertile, moist spot; given these conditions it is usually a plant of much beauty.

Also for that shady spot where plenty of moisture can be supplied, there is nothing that will give as much color as the fancy-leaf caladiums. Use a soil about the same as you would for ferns —lots of humus, a little plant food, plenty of water and that's all. More and more, fancy-leaved caladiums are coming into use for summer color. With the many new named varieties, you can work out very effective color combinations. The white-leaved ones are especially striking in front of evergreens or dark walls.

Throughout the South another planting of gladiolus may be made this month; in fact we may make one planting early in the month and still another late in the month. Several plantings will give us flowers over a much longer period. To prevent crooked stems, tie your gladiolus to small stakes. A simple way to handle rows of gladiolus is to drive small stakes at each end of the row and nail short crossarms, about six to eight inches long, to the stakes. Then run wires or strong cords from the ends of one arm to the ends of the other. The flower stem can be easily tied to the cords or wires.

In liriope we have found something for which we have been searching for a long time, a dependable evergreen edging plant that attains a height of six to ten inches. It is neat in appearance and in summer sends up spikes of lovely lavender flowers. It is perfectly hardy, thrives in sun or shade, and is not at all expensive. Monroi is a white-flowered variety.

Many of the tropical water lilies, which may be planted in most areas this month, are much more showy than the hardy types. Giant in size, their brilliant blooms persist throughout the growing season. If you plant only one water lily, it is a good idea to choose a tropical.

For that open, sunny slope or rock garden, *Phlox subulata* is the perfect subject. Rose, pink, white or red, its sheets of flowers cover the soil and foliage; with care, it remains persistent through the years. Grown from cuttings, divisions or roots, it must have plenty of water and good drainage.

If you have a southern slope that requires planting, try the purple-flowered or white varieties of *Desmodium*. Their graceful drooping branches adapt themselves to such situations. Although they die to the ground in winter, if given care and water they return each spring.

There are several things you can plant in **the vegetable garden** this month. Even up into the Middle South (Zone 8), plant bush and pole beans, lima beans, beets, carrots, corn, cucumbers, cantaloupes, endive, kale, English peas, (it is a little late now for lettuce), mustard, turnips, squash, black-eyed peas and crowder peas. Put out plants of peppers, tomatoes, eggplants and sweet potatoes. In the Upper South (Zone 7) it is not too late to plant Irish potatoes if you do it right away.

Why not border the flower beds with such practical crops as carrots, onions and lettuce? We find that it does not look bad at all. In fact, if the work is neatly done the effect will be quite pleasing. It is even possible to mix a few vegetables in with the perennials without lessening their beauty.

Ever try growing sweet potatoes in hills, like melons? Prepare the holes about thirty inches across and thirty inches deep, using plenty of leaf mold and a little well-rotted cow manure if available. Space the hills about six feet apart and plant four or five slips about a foot apart in each hill. The sweet potato is one of the best plants for shading out Bermuda and nut grass. You'll probably be surprised, too, at the number of nice potatoes you get from even a single hill tucked back in a corner somewhere.

FEEDING AND PRUNING

If you failed to fertilize the **daffodils** before they bloomed, do it now, while the foliage is still green. Bone meal, or a half-and-half mixture of bone meal and balanced plant food, is good for this purpose.

Both camellias and azaleas do practically all their growing in a very few weeks of spring, and any food applied should be given right after the blooms fade to benefit the plants during this spring growing season.

Spring-flowering shrubs should be pruned and fed just as the flowers have faded. (Summer-flowering species should have been pruned in February, of course.) If, after a severe winter, you find that some plants have been winterkilled, cut out the damaged wood back to sound growth. Badly damaged canes should be removed entirely.

Pick faded flowers from **English daisies and pansies**, apply liquid fertilizer every two or three weeks, water when needed, and they will continue in bloom for several weeks yet.

Lawns should be carefully checked early this month. Look for bad spots caused by disease, insects or severe weather. Repair damaged areas at once. At this season you should get good coverage in a very short time. Give at least one spring feeding.

In planting *Zoysia matrella*, one of the finest grasses for shady areas, be sure to work the soil especially well and keep the planting watered if there is a shortage of rainfall. Centipede grass has shown up very well in our own test plot, with much better growth in poor, neglected soils than any other grass we have tried, although one adverse report has been received from central Texas. For moderate or extreme shade we find St. Augustine very good also. (See Chapter 23.)

CONTROL OF PESTS AND DISEASE

Early this month there is usually a heavy infestation of **aphids** on the evergreen and semievergreen daylilies. All foliage carried through the winter should be trimmed off and the plants sprayed with a good insecticide. Be sure to turn the sprayer nozzle to force the chemical right down into the crowns of the plants. If the new foliage is already heavy, two people may be required to do the spraying job, one to hold the leaves back and another to apply the spray. Aphids on daylilies can easily spoil your most highly prized blooms by causing them to be distorted. Right now is the time to get rid of these insects.

Roses should be in full growth now, and there should be much good bloom by the end of the month. Our greatest problem in growing roses in the South is **black spot**. It cannot be "cured" but may be kept under control by using a good fungicide regularly. Don't be continually switching from one remedy to another; select a reliable preparation and stick with it. Use according to directions and you should have little trouble. Your garden store should have several dependable brands of fungicides. Avoid watering roses late in the afternoon, because moisture on the plants at night may encourage the spread of black spot. (See Chapter 22.)

Throughout the South azaleas have been attacked by the **lace bug**. These insects are very injurious; badly infested plants look unsightly and make little growth. Frosty, grayish appearance of the upper surface of the leaves indicates their presence. April is a good time to apply the first insecticide spray.

All of our well-laid plans for the home orchard will come to naught, insofar as the peaches and plums are involved, if steps are not taken this month to check the little **curculios** that cause wormy fruit. Spraying or dusting at this season is positively essential in order to have fruit free from worms. If only a few trees are involved, dusting will require less effort. The first application, either spray or dust, should be applied when about three fourths of the flower petals have fallen, and a second one about ten days later. If rains wash off the poison, make another application at once. Consult your seed store, co-op or county agent.

PLANTING LIST FOR APRIL

Seeds

Ageratum
Alyssum
Amaranthus
Anchusa
Arctotis
Baby blue-eyes
  (Nemophila)
Baby's-breath
  (Gypsophila)
Balsam (Impatiens)
Blue laceflower
  (Trachymene or
  Didiscus)
Calliopsis
Candytuft (Iberis)
Chinese
  forget-me-not
  (Cynoglossum)

Clarkia
Cleome
Cockscomb
  (Celosia)
Cosmos
Dahlia
Dimorphotheca
Feverfew
Gaillardia
Gourds, ornamental
Linaria
Lobelia
Marigold
Nasturtium
Nicotiana
Nierembergia

Pentstemon
Periwinkle
  (*Vinca rosea*)
Petunia
Platycodon
Portulaca
Salpiglossis
Salvia
Scabiosa
Strawflower
  (Helichrysum)
Sunflower
Torenia
Wallflower
  (Cheiranthus)
Zinnia

Bulbs, Rhizomes and Tubers

Achimenes
Allium
Billbergia
Blackberry lily
  (Belamcanda)
Butterfly lily
  (Hedychium)
Caladium
Calla lily
  (Zantedeschia)
Canna
Climbing lily
  (Gloriosa)

Crinum
Dahlia
Daylily
  (Hemerocallis)
Ginger lily
  (Zingiber)
Gladiolus
Habranthus
Hosta
Ismene
Jacobaean lily
  (Sprekelia)

Liriope
Montbretia
Oxalis
Rain lily
  (Zephyranthes)
Red-hot poker
  (Kniphofia)
Spider lily
  (Hymenocallis)
Tigridia
Tuberose
Watsonia

5

May

In the South, spring is the best time for making new lawns and for repairing bad spots in old ones. This is the most vigorous growing season, and there is usually more moisture in the soil than later in the season. In repairing you may seed, sprig or sod solid, but be sure to work up the soil and fertilize it well before doing the planting. After planting, keep well watered until ample new growth has developed.

If you are in a hurry to get the garden started, check at the plant and garden centers for bedding plants already growing. Of course, most of us could have easily had all the plants we needed if seed had been planted at the proper time, but May is here now, and we need to get the garden going without any further delay.

Many of the garden stores offer lovely bedding plants either in flats, trays or individual peat pots. The plants grown in trays are usually a bit cheaper than those in individual pots and are fine if you get them when they are still quite small, and if the root systems have not become so entwined that they will suffer great loss when the plants are removed from the trays. If the plants are overgrown with their root systems badly woven together, individually grown plants would be far better. As the season gets hotter, and perhaps drier, the importance of using started plants with good root systems becomes greater. I am especially sold on the little peat pots that permit the roots to grow right through the walls.

Have you pruned all of your spring-flowering shrubs? It might be well to check the entire planting to make sure. Early pruning results in more wood growth, which results in more flowers next spring. (See Chapter 24.)

All shrubs and evergreens should be generously fed at least once each season. You had better check for this also, and if you failed to feed any plants earlier in the season, do it now. Summer-flowering shrubs like altheas, crape myrtles and a few others form their flowers on new wood and should be fed this month to encourage the production of more growth, which means more flowers.

Check azaleas, camellias, roses and other things to see that ample mulches have been provided. Most young trees, too, will be much happier during the long, hot, dry summers if they are given a heavy mulch of straw or leaves.

In the Rio Grande Valley, along the Gulf Coast and in most of Florida (Zone 9), summer cuttings of many species of shrubs may be taken late this month. Most of the broad-leaf evergreens, including azaleas, camellias and boxwoods, will have wood that is sufficiently mature for rooting by the end of the month. May is also my favorite month for air layering. (See Chapter 25.)

We should all know by this time not to remove the foliage from the daffodils, tulips and other spring-flowering bulbs until it has matured. You may pull the foliage down and partially cover it with soil, pleat it together, or do almost anything you wish except remove it. Just as a rose bush must have its foliage for manufacturing food, so must the daffodil—without leaves it cannot survive.

WHAT TO PLANT

In the Middle South (Zone 8) we may plant even the tenderest summer annuals without fear of frost. If you have more seeds to plant, go ahead and get them into the soil as soon as con-

venient. All the way from East Texas to the Atlantic Coast, plant
now in the open seeds of such heat-lovers as amaranthus, balsam,
cockscomb, marigold, portulaca and zinnia.

Annual vines may still be planted. (See Chapter 26.)

From East Texas, across Louisiana, Mississippi, Alabama and
Georgia, chrysanthemums, daisies, physostegia, phlox and many
other **perennials** should have immediate attention if they have
not already been separated and replanted. Continue setting out
chrysanthemum plants of all types. (See Chapter 16.)

May is a good time to plant many **summer-flowering bulbous
things**: caladiums, cannas, dahlias, spider lilies, ismenes, montbretias, red-hot pokers, summer hyacinths, tigridias, tropical
water lilies, zephyranthes and many others. Although others in
the South have grown them successfully, summer hyacinths
(*Galtonia candicans*) have never survived for more than two
seasons with me.

Montbretias are lovely flowers that are easily grown—too easily
perhaps; they increase rapidly in good soil and may soon get out
of bounds.

Have you grown gloriosas? Everyone seems to love these
climbing lilies, but relatively few gardeners grow them. Our
clump of the rothschildsiana type attracts more attention when
in bloom than anything else around. It is not too late to plant,
but do it right away.

Make an additional planting of gladiolus every two weeks this
month and next. Give plenty of moisture, as the flower stems are
developing.

Hemerocallis will be at their best in most areas this month and
next. Call them daylilies, if you like, but let's not confuse ourselves and our friends by calling them "lilies." They are definitely
not lilies, and we confuse people when we give them that name.
The daylily is assuredly one of our most popular garden flowers,
and its popularity is increasing each season. Visit all the shows
you can, as well as the open gardens. See the plants in bloom
and make notes of the ones you will want to plant a little later.
Daylilies will tolerate a lot of dry weather, but they should have
plenty of moisture during their flowering season, beginning when

the scapes start developing and continuing until the season ends.

The water is warm enough now for the tropical lilies to go into the pool. These tropicals bloom from early summer until late fall without a break and are much superior to the hardy types, many of which bloom only in the spring.

Feeding the fish in the pool regularly will go a long way in keeping them in good health and will result in more rapid propagation. Oatmeal is a very good food, but prepared fish food, which may be found at the feed stores, is better, as it contains animal matter.

The length of time required to bring a seedling amaryllis to bloom depends largely on the care given, but do not expect much bloom until the third year; after that, they should not only bloom every year but multiply rapidly. If you grow amaryllis from seed, be sure to give the seedlings good soil and water them during the dry seasons. I believe a partially shaded location is best for the young plants.

Amaryllis may be left undivided for four or five years. Our five-year-old clumps are sending up as many as eight scapes and developing twenty flowers to the clump. After the flowers fade, growth slows down for a while, and that is a good time to make new plantings and to separate and replant old clumps. Inasmuch as they will not be disturbed for several years, try to do a good job of planting. The hole for each bulb should be eighteen inches deep and as wide. Equal parts of sand, peat moss and soil make a good mixture for them. The usual recommendation is that the bulbs be planted in the South at such a depth that after the soil has settled the shoulders of the bulbs will be covered but the necks left above the soil level. Keep your bulbs covered until planted; never permit the fresh roots to dry out. In the Middle South (Zone 8) they will need a heavy mulch of straw for winter protection.

Red fire (*Stagnosa curtisii*) is a disease that attacks amaryllis and may actually destroy the bulbs. It is indicated by a reddish rust that attacks the leaves and flower stems, "eating" through and causing them to fall to the ground. Digging the bulbs annually and soaking for twenty-four hours in a spray-strength solution of any good fungicide, then watering them with the same solution, seems to do much to keep the disease under control.

CONTROL OF PESTS AND DISEASE

Here in the South the campaign for control of insects and diseases must be waged relentlessly from early spring until frost arrives, and best garden practice calls for a few sprayings even during the winter months. While we have some bugs throughout the year, it is during the spring months that their hordes increase. Sprays and dusts are far more effective if applied when the insects are young. Taken as a whole, May is perhaps the most important month for killing insects.

There are many remedies on the market, and several are all-purpose for the control of both insects and diseases. My good Woman Friday sometimes mixes insecticides and fungicides to furnish an all-purpose spray, with very good results. Not all remedies are compatible, however, and you had better check before mixing them. Do not let the great number of new preparations being ballyhooed in the magazines and over the air confuse you. If you have a neighbor who is a successful gardener, talk to her, or go to your garden supply store for advice. A reliable dealer will always give you dependable information on what to use. Select a good fungicide and one insecticide and stick to them, at least for the season. While there are a few insects, like ants, snails and scale, that require special remedies, a good general insecticide should control 90 percent of the bugs that damage your plants and flowers.

May is one of the best months for killing **weeds** with the new chemicals. Practically all plant life is growing vigorously this month, and that's the way you need it for best results. These chemicals are sold under various trade names and formulations. For application, try to pick a still day. Wind can cause drift of the poisons and damage to other things besides the weeds.

Crab grass is a hot-weather pest; the seeds do not germinate until the soil gets thoroughly warm. Use both pre-emergency chemicals and special crab-grass killers this month.

This is the season for **pillbugs, snails and slugs.** You will find effective poisons at your local seed store or you may consult your county agent. Aphids cause serious damage to daylily flower buds just as the scapes push through the crown. Spray this month with a dependable insecticide. The spray should also control cucumber beetles, which sometimes attack the daylily blooms.

Spraying the trunks of young dogwood trees this month with any good insecticide will do much to ward off attacks by **borers.** Many young dogwoods are killed by these insects, which enter the trunks near the ground, bore to the center of the trunk and then tunnel upwards.

Borers of various kinds entering the stalks of plants are often a problem. One way to eradicate them is by packing a tiny piece of cotton dipped in nicotine sulphate into the hole in the stalk, using a toothpick or a match. The fumes kill the worms.

If troubled with **cutworms** or other night feeders, as most of us are this month, try placing a piece of old linoleum or boards on the ground near the plants. Look under these in the morning and you'll find many prowlers waiting to be liquidated.

Give the azaleas and camellias a second application of miscible oil. Apply this spray also to other shrubs such as peaches, lilacs and gardenias, which are susceptible to attacks by **scale.**

Many gardenias develop a sooty **black mold** during late spring, which may do serious damage to the plants. It is caused by a honeydew left by insects. The mold is not parasitic and within itself draws no nourishment from the plants, but it does shut off light, thus interfering with photosynthesis and the manufacture of food in the leaves.

Garden authorities tell us now that the easiest way to rid our grounds of **moles** is first to rid the garden soil of worms and grubs on which the moles feed. Ask your garden supplier for a good preparation for this purpose.

Wherever azaleas are grown in the South, **lace bugs** always seem to be present. Two sprayings annually—April or May and September—will usually keep them under control.

PLANTING LIST FOR MAY

Seeds

Ageratum
Amaranthus
Anchusa
Baby blue-eyes
 (Nemophila)
Baby's-breath
 (Gypsophila)
Balsam
 (Impatiens)
Blue laceflower
 (Trachymene or
 Didiscus)
Calliopsis
China aster
Clarkia
Cleome
Clitoria

Cockscomb
 (Celosia)
Cosmos
Dahlia
Feverfew
Gaillardia
Linaria
Linum
Lobelia
Marigold
Mignonette
Moonflower
 (Calonyction)
Morning glory
Nicotiana
Nierembergia

Periwinkle
 (*Vinca rosea*)
Petunia
Platycodon
Portulaca
Salpiglossis
Salvia
Scabiosa
Strawflower
 (Helichrysum)
Sunflower
Tithonia
Torenia
Wallflower
 (Cheiranthus)
Zinnia

Bulbs, Rhizomes and Tubers

Achimenes
Billbergia
Butterfly lily
 (Hedychium)
Caladium
Calla lily
 (Zantedeschia)
Canna
Climbing lily
 (Gloriosa)

Dahlia
Daylily
 (Hemerocallis)
Ginger lily
 (Zingiber)
Gladiolus
Habranthus
Hosta
Liriope

Montbretia
Nerine
Oxalis
Rain lily
 (Zephyranthes)
Tigridia
Tuberose
Water lily

6

June

You may continue repairing old and making new lawns during June, using seed, sod or sprigging, as the situation warrants. If you have a crab-grass problem, talk to the manager of your garden store. Remember that all recently planted or repaired lawns should have an ample supply of food and moisture for the next few months to get them off to a good start.

Give the house plants a vacation this summer by plunging the containers to the rims in soil outdoors in a semishady part of the garden. You'd better turn the pots every month or two to prevent roots growing through the drainage hole and deeply into the soil below.

Newly planted boxwoods, camellias and gardenias should have some shade during the hot summer months. Old established plants of these species may be able to stand the sun, but young plants will many times suffer unless given a little protection.

Do not forget to check the mulches, especially those on the shrubs of various kinds and the perennial and fall-blooming annuals. Just about everything we grow in the Deep South will be happier with a good summer mulch except the bearded irises and the Shasta-type daisies; these two should never be mulched. (See Chapter 28.)

Stake cosmos, tithonias, lilies and chrysanthemums, if this has

43

not already been done. June is an important month in the culture of all types of chrysanthemums. (See Chapter 16.)

WHAT TO PLANT

Just as soon as the flowers in the hardy annual beds have faded, clean them out for another crop. Cornflowers, California and annual poppies, larkspurs, gaillardias and phlox have nearly spent themselves now. Clean out the beds thoroughly, work and enrich the soil and sow **summer annuals;** there are many from which to choose. With the soil and air both warm, the plants will grow like all outdoors and will give you a mass of flowers in a few short weeks. You'll then have material for filling in the bad spots in the beds a little later on. And if your place is like mine, there are always bad spots.

You will hardly find a better annual for hot, dry spots than the old periwinkle (*Vinca rosea*); it will also do well in moderate shade and where the soil is a bit on the moist side. The border type Coquette is compact and bushy, growing only about ten inches high. Here is a real beauty, and it is not too late to plant it in the Middle South (Zone 8).

June is not too early to plant seeds of **biennials,** but success may be had with most species planted any time during the summer months. Foxgloves reseed beautifully. We now have scores of seedlings in the beds where we had the flowers last year. We plan to move these little plants to a growing bed or to the permanent places in the garden as soon as we can find time. A new hybrid foxglove is one of the prettiest and most spectacular of flowers, and nothing is easier to grow. Why do we not see more of them?

The Elbert Wards of Jackson, Mississippi, successful growers of fine irises, advise that June is perhaps the best month of all for planting **bearded irises** in the South, and my experience bears them out. June planting gives the irises an opportunity to become established before the season for forming flower buds arrives. It will definitely give you stronger plants for next spring's bloom than if you waited until late summer or fall to put them in. Old plantings may also be dug and reset, where that is in order. Bearded, Louisiana, Oriental and Siberian types may be planted this month. Ever try growing the Siberian in huge clumps? Very effective.

Much transplanting will be done this month. The weather is sure to be hot and will probably be dry. If you are growing your seedlings in plant bands or small pots, they will suffer practically no shock in transplanting. Most garden stores carry both bands and pots. Quart milk cartons cut in sections two and a half inches high make excellent bands. Place them on a stiff board, fill with growing soil and set one plant in each band. My good Woman Friday just bought a hundred small clay pots (three inches) and finds them a great convenience in handling chrysanthemum plants from the time they are well rooted until she is ready to place them in the permanent beds.

If you buy container-grown plants—that is, grown in cans—be sure to have the nurseryman slit the side of the can so that the earth may be removed intact. If the ball of earth cracks badly, countless little feed roots will be destroyed. By proper handling, **container-grown shrubs and roses** may be planted right on through the summer. Be sure to keep them well watered, however.

Butterfly bush, flowering senna (cassia), cestrum, duranta, justicia and plumbago may be transplanted from pots, or moved successfully, if the holes are filled with water, the ground around the plants kept soaked for several days, and the plants well shaded until they recover from the shock. These plants will give excellent summer and autumn bloom. (See Chapter 24.)

There are many **bulbous things** you can plant this month. If you can get dormant material, so much the better. Amazon lily, billbergia, caladium, canna, climbing lily, dahlia, habranthus, hosta, liriope, lycoris and zephyranthes should do well planted now if kept watered.

In those deep shady spots where most things do not grow well, the fancy-leaf caladium is still a good bet. Given shade, plenty of fertilizer and water, it will give you a great show. You can get different colors in named varieties or plants from the garden stores already growing.

June is about the only month that lycoris is thoroughly dormant, and this is the best time to handle this plant. The foliage should be dead now, but it will be only a few weeks before the roots begin growing again, to send up new flower stalks in August and September. Plant lycoris bulbs very shallowly, with the neck above the soil line. Deep planting is probably the reason that many of these bulbs do not bloom well.

June is a good month for planting dahlias for fall bloom. Many of the prize winners at the shows are planted now.

If you do not like the ungainly appearance of your cannas, remove the flower stems after the first crop of flowers has faded. Your beds will look neater and you may gain much additional growth and bloom.

Do not pass up an opportunity to see the new daylilies in bloom. It is far better to see them in bloom and make your selections than to depend on color reproductions and descriptions from the catalog. Actually, true colors of these flowers are difficult to reproduce and you could easily be misled by such pictures.

In the vegetable garden, harvest all crops that have finished for the year and replant immediately. There is time to grow another crop of nearly all the leafy vegetables, beans, peas, corn, tomatoes, cucumbers and melons. It is not too late to put out plants of peppers, eggplants and sweet potatoes. Summer-planted seeds should be planted a little deeper than those planted in the spring; and, unless drainage is poor, level cultivation is usually better than planting in ridges.

PRUNING

Most of the spring-flowering shrubs produce flowers on second-year wood—that is, next spring's flowers will be grown on wood produced this season. These shrubs should be pruned rather severely right after all flowers have faded, in order to give time for production of wood for next season's flowers. Spring-flowering shrubs that bloom late, like deutzias, weigelas and some mock oranges (Philadelphus), should be cut back severely right after they finish blooming. If this was not done earlier, I'd wait no longer. Do not give the shrub a "flat top" in pruning, but remove some of the old canes down to different lengths so the new growth will be distributed over the plant and not concentrated at the top. (See Chapter 24.)

If you find dying branches among your azaleas, check for split bark. Cut dying branches down to sound wood.

There are several different types of climbing roses, and each requires different cultural treatment, especially in the matter of pruning. To be able to handle them properly we should study the different types in order to give them their particular type of treatment. Roses of the true climber type, like Dr. W. Van Fleet and Silver Moon, may be pruned lightly this season. All dead and unhealthy wood should be removed and the canes cut back, if they are getting out of bounds.

FEEDING

All through the year I receive inquiries about feeding **shrubs and young trees.** Early spring, just as the leaf buds begin to grow, is definitely the best time to feed these plants in the South, but if you failed to feed them then it is not too late. I would, however, make it a point to feed them right away, as in the South it is not good practice to fertilize shrubs later than midsummer.

Food and moisture can work wonders on plants. If you have shrubs and young trees that have lost their vigor and seem to care little whether they live or die, try giving them a heavy feeding of high-grade plant food and plenty of water—unless, of course, there is ample rain.

Most **lawns** should be fed this month, using about half as much plant food as you used in February. An early summer feeding of shrubs and trees will give better growth, but as a rule I give just one heavy feeding when I do the pruning in February and do not feed again that season.

Proper care of **peonies** is necessary for next year's bloom. Dry blooms should be cut off, during this month, and a complete fertilizer used around each plant. It is during the summer months that peonies form their growing "eyes" for next year, and the plants will need food and water in order to make proper development.

If you want continuous bloom from your **floribunda roses,** be sure to keep the faded flower heads removed, feed the plants regularly and see that they get plenty of moisture. The floribundas will need, of course, the same regular applications of fungicides that you give your other roses.

Keep all faded flowers cut from the **annuals and perennials.** Give light cultivation and feed with liquid fertilizer.

PLANT PROPAGATION

May and June are fine months for **layering** plants. Most of those that make wiry growth, like the jasmines, honeysuckles and climbing roses, are easily layered. (See Chapter 25.)

Last season I found that top grafts on camellias placed in June grew just about as well as those made in February. If you have any **grafting** you wish to do, I suggest you try it now. For scions we used the exact type of wood as used for summer cuttings, but the pieces were cut a bit short.

You may make stump or cleft grafts of camellias this month but may not get any growth until next spring. Sometimes June and July grafts will start growing right away, but at other times (maybe the variety has something to do with it) they make no growth until the following spring. We made a stump graft of a very valuable camellia on one Fourth of July. The scion remained green but made no growth whatever until May of the next year. Cleft grafts made in summer should be watered occasionally if the weather is dry, to prevent their drying out before a union can be formed. A handful of sphagnum moss wrapped around the graft and kept moist will do much to supply needed humidity.

June is the month for taking summer or **softwood cuttings** of all sorts—deciduous shrubs, broad-leaf and narrow-leaf evergreens. The main point is to provide good drainage and a very tight covering that will hold moisture. The modern sheet plastic is ideal, as it permits a circulation of air but prevents the escape of moisture. For containers you may use anything from coffee cans, punched for drainage, to flats or elaborate cutting beds. (See Chapter 25.) If cuttings will root at all, you should be able to do it this month.

CONTROL OF PESTS AND DISEASE

The scientists are working fast; every year we see new plant foods, new insecticides and new fungicides placed on the market. The newer rooting chemical chromosomes are claimed to be superior to anything of the kind previously introduced.

Check the chrysanthemums. **Leaf spot** usually makes its appearance this month on the ones planted early, and of course we have been fighting it on the roses since March.

Last year, before we realized what was taking place, some insect badly damaged a number of buds on our gloriosas. They are so lovely and exotic that we are grieved at losing even one flower. Spraying at ten-day intervals with a good insecticide, from the time the buds begin to show until the flowers open, should give complete protection.

During June, when most plants are still in luscious growth, is a good time to use the chemical **weed killers.** All of the ones I have tried are good, but a few are very selective: they will kill plants of one species but not those of another. Two seasons ago I received samples of poison ivy killer and as an experiment applied some of it on a bed containing, among other things, much poison ivy, Japanese honeysuckle, worthless daylily seedlings, English ivy and numerous and sundry weeds. The poison ivy died quickly and has not shown up again, but all the other plants, after looking quite sick for several weeks, came back to life. Because of this selectivity and the danger of the spray mist's drifting to nearby plants and injuring them, all these chemical killers should be applied strictly as directed by the manufacturer.

Even though you have had no trouble with **scale,** spray the camellias again this month, using either miscible oil, at summer strengtn, or a reliable insecticide. In order to keep the azaleas clear of **lace bugs,** a second spraying for them is in order this month.

Mildew is sometimes a problem with crape myrtles, verbenas, zinnias, perennial phlox and other species of plants. None of the old remedies has been entirely successful, but now there are some new ones at your seed and plant stores that are quite effective. Ask about them.

PLANTING LIST FOR JUNE

Seeds

Balsam
  (Impatiens)
Blue laceflower
  (Trachymene or
  Didiscus)
Clarkia
Cleome
Clitoria
Cockscomb
  (Celosia)
Coleus
Cosmos

Cypress vine
Feverfew
Gaillardia
Marigold
Mignonette
Moonflower
  (Calonyction)
Morning glory
Nicotiana
Periwinkle
  (*Vinca rosea*)
Platycodon

Portulaca
Salpiglossis
Scabiosa
Strawflower
  (Helichrysum)
Sunflower
Tithonia
Torenia
Wallflower
  (Cheiranthus)
Zinnia

Bulbs, Rhizomes and Tubers

Amazon lily
  (Eucharis)
Billbergia
Butterfly lily
  (Hedychium)
Caladium
Canna
Climbing lily
  (Gloriosa)

Dahlia
Ginger lily
  (Zingiber)
Habranthus
Hosta
Iris
  Bearded
  Japanese
  Louisiana
  Siberian

Liriope
Lycoris
Rain lily
  (Zephyranthes)
Tuberose
Water lily

7

July

Clean up in July: Remove spent annual flowers from the beds and prune back the perennials to make room for the second crop of annuals, which, planted now, should give good bloom during September and October. It is a good idea to always have some young seedlings coming on to fill the vacant spaces where spent flowers have been removed, but if you do not want to go to the trouble of growing them, you will find at the garden stores lots of little things growing in individual pots which may easily be transferred to the garden beds. If you buy plants growing in little peat pots, be sure to get the rim of the pots under the surface of the soil; otherwise they will dry out, harden, and retard growth of the plants.

You can improve the appearance of your garden, and at the same time increase bloom, by clipping back some of the plants that have been blooming for a long time. Try shearing such things as alyssum, candytuft, nepeta, verbena, phlox and physostegia.

Induce such summer-flowering plants as crape myrtle, althea and vitex to continue blooming over a longer period by removing the faded flower heads, cultivating lightly and seeing that the plants are well fed and watered.

Do not permit the Shasta-type daisies to overcrowd, especially during this season of great heat and occasional summer showers. Overcrowding with too much heat and moisture will cause the plants to rot. Give all daisies good drainage, air circulation and sunshine.

Dutch irises, tulips and gladiolus may be dug as soon as the foliage has turned a deep yellow. Let the bulbs cure in the shade for a few days; then clean and store them in the basement or other cool, dry place.

July is a trying month for dahlias. Try to keep them growing by feeding them occasionally and giving them plenty of water. Once a dahlia is stunted, it never regains its full vigor. Cut back early planted dahlias to induce new growth for fall flowers. If you can get the tubers, make additional plantings this month. Many of the blue-ribbon takers at the fall shows are from tubers planted in June and July. Feed and water when needed.

This is the month when many rose growers give their plants a rest. From early July until about late August, no food or water is applied and blooming is discouraged by picking off the flower buds. About the last of August a very, very light pruning is given, the excess twigs are clipped out and perhaps a little top growth removed; a double dose of plant food and plenty of water should be given. And what wonderful fall roses are produced!

Occasionally a budded rose will produce a sprout from the rootstock, but these wild shoots are easily identified by the difference in foliage. Remove the earth for an inch or two at the base of the plant and cut off the offending cane flush with a sharp knife.

If you plan to move your daffodils this summer do it right away, as the roots will begin growing on many varieties next month. It is not necessary to move daffodils every year, but if it is to be done this summer, July and August are good months for the job.

WHAT TO PLANT

Our best fall **annuals** are grown from summer planted seed. Right now is the time to make a heavy planting of seeds of ageratum, alyssum, calliopsis, cockscomb, cosmos, gaillardia, marigold, portulaca, torenia and zinnia. Locate the bed in partial shade, but with good light. The soil should be deep and fertile.

One of the oldest seed houses in the country reports that a survey indicates an increase in the amount of annual seeds being used each season but that seeds of fewer perennial flowers are being planted now. Both types of flowers should be used. If the gardener does not use perennials, he's missing a number of the best flower varieties to augment his display of annuals. Perennials provide different colors and plant types with bloom earlier than most annuals. July is a good month to plant seed of both **biennials and perennials.** Some of the best to grow are: achillea, dianthus, columbine, foxglove, gloriosa daisy, daisy and Sweet William. Plant in a deep fertile soil, and in partial shade, and see that the seedlings get plenty of moisture and food.

A liberal quantity of coarse sand and peat moss mixed into the soil for your seedbeds will improve its texture and encourage root growth on the young seedlings. This mixture will also cling to the roots of the seedlings when they are transplanted from the bed and enable you to move them with less shock. We always use one of the root-inducing chemicals, like Transplantone, in transplanting small garden plants.

July is the beginning of the main season for planting **daylilies,** but it extends until late fall. Of all plants, hemerocallis is one of the easiest to handle. While in bloom, clumps may be lifted with balls of earth and moved to strategic points in the beds to give proper color effects. Water them well after moving and all will be well. We once received a shipment by express, dug with bare roots while in bloom. They were a week in transportation but had not stopped blooming. Several plants had open blooms when received.

Daylilies that have finished blooming may now be divided and replanted, if that is to be done this season.

The iris planting season, which begins in June, extends right on through the summer and fall. Other bulbous things you may plant this month include Amazon lily, billbergia, habranthus, water lily, liriope, lycoris, zephyranthes and many irises.

It is getting a bit late to plant lycoris, but there is still time if you hurry. Some seasons lycoris fail to bloom, and many growers attribute the failure to letting the beds get too dry. Although lack of adequate moisture may be involved in many cases, this is not always the trouble. Planting too deep is perhaps the greatest cause of failure to bloom. The bulbs should be barely covered with earth.

Caladiums, like chrysanthemums, are a year-round crop for most florists, and home gardeners in the South may have them from spring until late fall. If you can locate sound corms that have been kept in cool storage and plant them this month, they should make a brilliant showing until frost. These plants are ideal for that shady spot where few other things will grow. Be sure to give them plenty of moisture.

From Houston across to New Orleans and eastward, keep things growing **in the vegetable garden** the year round. This month plant cabbage, cauliflower, celery, broccoli, Brussels sprouts, parsnips, peas, beans and the leafy vegetables. If the spring-planted things have matured, pull them out, prepare the soil and plant another crop.

There is now on the market a plant hormone which, if sprayed on tomato plants while in bloom, tends to take the place of pollen and gives a better fall crop. Fall production of this vegetable is often poor because of imperfect pollination; the hormone helps correct that trouble.

Most gardeners prefer to prune and stake their tomatoes, as they will then require less space. But unpruned plants usually produce more fruit, and, although it may be slightly smaller than from pruned plants, it is sometimes preferred for canning and general table use. Unpruned, unstaked plants should have a mulch placed around them to protect the fruit when the plants sprawl over.

PLANT PRUNING AND PROPAGATION

While the season for rooting **summer cuttings** is a long one, I like June and early July best. To root quickly, the cuttings must have heat and a high degree of humidity, so keep them tightly closed until the roots begin to form. Keep the rooting medium moist but not soggy. (See Chapter 25.)

Early July is considered a good time for cutting back both outdoor- and indoor-grown **poinsettias**. Pruned now, they should branch well and give much more bloom. Treated as other summer cuttings, these prunings from the poinsettias are easily rooted.

The "books" used to tell us that we could prune **azaleas** as late as July first, but by experimenting over a number of years I have determined that on my grounds this is much too late. Pruned July first, fed and watered, they should make nice new growth, but much of it will not form flower buds and there is also danger of this late tender new growth being winterkilled. Unless the plants are getting out of bounds, I would not prune now; wait until the flowers fade next spring and then prune immediately. (See Chapter 19.) However, the long branchless canes sometimes found in the fast-growing azaleas at this season should be cut back to the general contour of the plant. This will greatly improve the appearance of the plants and result in more flowers.

FEEDING AND WATERING

Feed the **lawn** this month and see that it gets plenty of moisture. Cut the grass only moderately close. Dry weather, hot sun and cutting too close may cause your grass to die out. While the usual cause of yellowing of St. Augustine grass is chinch bugs, it is sometimes caused from lack of iron. The trouble can usually be corrected by sprinkling the yellowed area with a solution of copperas, using a tablespoonful of the powdered material to each gallon of water; or iron chelates may be used. If one sprinkling does not result in the proper change in color, make another application in two or three weeks.

Most of the heavy-foliaged **broad-leaved plants** lose much moisture by transpiration during the summer when the weather is dry, and unless there is sufficient moisture in the soil to offset the loss, serious injury may result. Watch such plants as azaleas, aucubas, camellias, gardenias, loquats and the hollies to see that they do not get too dry. The best test is to examine the soil; do not wait until the plant wilts.

This month and next are very hard on trees and shrubs planted last season, especially shallow-rooted things like the azaleas, and all those planted late. See that they get ample water or some may die quickly.

On the first of June our **Magnolia soulangeanas** sometimes has flower buds an inch long, already formed for next spring's flowers. Many azaleas and camellias, especially the early varieties, are now in progress of forming flower buds. These species that form their buds so early should have ample moisture during this season. If they get too dry now the buds cannot properly develop and mature.

Pink rain lilies (zephyranthes) will show few blooms during the hot, dry summers unless they get an occasional soaking or heavy rain. One good wetting, however, will usually result in a mass of bloom within two or three days.

This is a good time to give the water lilies a little food. Wet the plant food, roll into pills and push them into the soil after they have dried. Or you can wrap the food in small pieces of cloth—a tablespoonful to the serving—and push it down into the soil. These methods of feeding get the food down near the roots of the plants and result in the least pollution of the water. If you didn't repot the plants in the spring, summer feeding is doubly important.

Your garden pool will lose much of its effectiveness if you let it become overcrowded with plants. Leave at least one third of the water's surface exposed. If necessary, cut out some of the oldest lily pads; it will help both the plants and the appearance of the pool.

CONTROL OF PESTS AND DISEASE

The waves of heat that pervade much of the South this month tend to lessen our interest in gardening, but they add to the vitality and vigor of a multitude of weeds. Force yourself to keep right after them; it is important not to let them go to seed. On the lawn, one of the chemical sprays will help. After a heavy rain (or a good soaking from the hose) is a good time to pull weeds from the flower beds.

It will be much easier to keep **cedar-apple rust** under control if you keep the "apples" removed from the red cedars and don't permit any of them to mature. This disease can easily prove disastrous to both native and many of the cultivated crabs. The Bechtel seems to be highly susceptible—ours was killed in a single season, although we sprayed constantly.

There are several all-purpose insecticides, many in dust form, at the seed stores now. Most of these insecticides are thoroughly dependable and will keep your plants free of nearly all diseases and of all insects.

Dogwoods, peaches, plums and some other trees are subject to attack by **borers**. The moths lay their eggs in the bark in summer and may be controlled by spraying the trunks and larger branches with a reliable insecticide. Two or three applications at ten-day intervals should be sufficient.

Bagworms attack several species of juniper and arborvitae at this season. They may practically defoliate nice junipers within a few days. After picking off the little bags and burning them, spray the plants with a dependable insecticide, making the solution about 50 percent stronger than for tender annuals.

Lace bugs attack azaleas and pyracanthas. Evidence of their presence is the frosty, grayish appearance of the upper surfaces of the leaves and brown specks on the undersides. Spraying with a dependable insecticide will check them.

This is the season for **red spiders**. These mites attack any number of plants, particularly arborvitaes, azaleas and phlox, and their presence may be indicated by a reddish stain left after you rub a leaf between finger and thumb. For control, consult your seed or plant store.

A certain amount of moisture is necessary for the development of fungus diseases; during hot dry weather they make little headway, and you may slow down on the use of fungicides unless rainy spells occur.

PLANTING LIST FOR JULY

Seeds

Achillea
Ageratum
Alyssum
Balsam
  (Impatiens)
Blue laceflower
  (Trachymene or
  Didiscus)
Calliopsis
Carnation
  (Dianthus)

Cleome
Clitoria
Cockscomb
  (Celosia)
Coleus
Cosmos, late
Foxglove
Gaillardia
Marigold
Mignonette

Moonflower
  (Calonyction)
Morning Glory
Portulaca
Strawflower
  (Helichrysum)
Sweet William
Tithonia
Torenia
Zinnia

Bulbs, Rhizomes and Tubers

Amazon lily
  (Eucharis)
Billbergia
Caladium
Dahlia
Daylily
  (Hemerocallis)
Ginger lily
  (Zingiber)

Habranthus
Iris
  Bearded
  Japanese
  Louisiana
  I. cristata
  I. unguicularis

Liriope
Lycoris
Rain lily
  (Zephyranthes)
Sternbergia
Water lily

8

August

The real test of a good gardener comes during the hot summer days, for just a little too much loafing and the garden soon matures and spends itself. Annuals and perennials cease to bloom and the weeds ripen their many seeds and spread them to plague us next spring. But just a little extra effort will tend to keep things blooming right through autumn and well into the winter. Clip back leggy plants, remove all faded flowers and seed pods, cultivate lightly among the plants, fertilize and water— plenty of water. I promise you satisfactory rewards.

Do not overlook the lawn. Hot, dry weather is hard on lawns, and cutting the grass short makes the situation much worse. Close cutting may actually kill out a well-established lawn; adjust the blades so as to leave the grass at least a half inch longer than for spring cutting. A little food and plenty of water will go a long way toward keeping the sod green during the trying summer months.

Right now is a good time to visit your local nursery or plant sales yard. The employees will have more time to talk to you and answer your questions about nursery stock. You will also be likely to find some real bargains—and remember, container-grown plants may be planted at any time.

Fill the bare spots in the borders (annuals, perennials and

shrubs) with seedlings of annuals. There is still plenty of time in most areas to get a good crop of blooms before frost arrives. If you don't care to bother with growing them, plants may be picked up at the garden stores.

Across the Middle South—Tyler, Marshall, Vicksburg, Jackson, Meridian and Montgomery and to the coast—it is time to procure seed of English daisies and pansies for planting later. An accepted date for making the first planting of these biennials or hardy annuals (they seem to fit either category) is Labor Day, so have your seed ready. If you do not wish bloom until spring, you may wait until early October to plant. Many gardeners make two plantings—one around Labor Day and another in October—for continuous winter and spring bloom. Double rows, one of English daisies and one of pansies, in mixed or solid colors, make a superb border for late winter and early spring. For the large or small garden, or for indoor decoration, these two plants have everything. They bloom before and with the azaleas and fit into the garden picture for the spring garden pilgrimages.

This is a good time to tidy up the rose bed. An amazing amount of nourishment goes into the production of seeds and fruits of the plants. Practically all plant life will grow better and bloom more profusely if the faded flowers and fruit capsules are regularly removed to prevent the formation of fruit. Floribunda roses, both bush and climbing forms, are strong in the production of capsules, or hips. The best practice is to remove the heads of flowers just as soon as they fade; if this is not done, lose no time in clipping off faded flowers and fruits.

WHAT TO PLANT

Don't let weeds take over the beds where spring annuals bloomed. If you have not already cleaned the beds, get at it immediately. After the soil is ready, plant a fall crop of annuals or transplant started plants to the beds. In the Rio Grande Valley, along the Gulf Coast and across Florida (Zone 9) most of the summer annuals may still be planted for September and October bloom. In fact, many of them, if planted now, even in the Middle

South (Zone 8), should make a good showing of bloom before cold weather arrives. Nor is it too early to plant balsam, calendula, cornflower, cosmos, marigold, vinca and zinnia seed for late fall and early winter bloom. But early this month is our last chance in the Upper South (Zone 7); there will hardly be time after the middle of the month.

If you grow **hollyhocks**, destroy all foliage and stalks just as soon as they have finished blooming. Plant fresh seed in July or August to get fresh disease-free plants for the following season. Rust is the worst enemy of hollyhocks; it appears in brownish pustules in the leaves. Old plants are hosts for the disease.

You'll probably be doing quite a lot of transplanting this month. Pick a cloudy day if possible. If the earth happens to be dry, make the hole for the plant and fill it with water. After the water has soaked in, place the plant, fill with soil, and water again. Most leggy annuals should be severely pinched back before being transplanted. Use one of the root-promoting hormones in transplanting and water with a weak solution of liquid fertilizer. If the weather is sunny, shade for a few days.

From Arkansas across to the Atlantic, August is a good time to divide and plant **Madonna and other lilies** that flower in the spring. They may be separated now if they are crowding. Practically all perennials on which the foliage has somewhat matured may be divided and planted, but they must be watered well after planting.

Daylilies which have finished flowering for the season may be separated and replanted now if crowded. Dig the whole clump, shake or wash off the earth, separate with a knife and cut back to about four or five inches. After planting, water well and they will soon establish themselves. This is also a good time to make new daylily plantings. One of the many fine things about this flower is that in the South it may be planted at almost any time. No garden flower will stand more neglect and abuse. If you are growing your daylilies from seed, remember to gather and plant them just as soon as the seed pods turn a deep yellow or light brown.

August is one of the best months for setting plants of most

irises. Continue planting bearded irises this month and next. The newer irises are very lovely and much superior to most of the old varieties. Just a few of them will add interest to your planting. If the weather is dry, water well as soon as the planting is finished. We are charmed with *Iris unguicularis*, which, with the right kind of weather, may be expected to bloom in the Middle South through December and January. Should a freeze kill back the flower scapes, only three or four moderately warm days are necessary for new flowers to appear. The stems are relatively short and the white or lilac blooms do not rival the huge ones of bearded irises that greet us in April, but they are highly prized, since they appear in midwinter.

August is also a good time to do something about the fall **vegetable plot** in the Middle South. Turnips, mustard, beets, carrots, peas, beans, collards and cabbage can be planted now. Late this month and through September put out strawberry plants. Old varieties like Blakemore and Klondike are still good. For the newer ones adapted to your locality consult your county agricultural agent.

WATERING AND FEEDING

Sometimes we have "dog day" showers all through August, but during most summers the month is both hot and dry. It is, perhaps, the most important month when it comes to artificial watering. Remember, always, it is much better to water thoroughly once each week than to sprinkle every day.

You can keep many of your **annuals** blooming several weeks longer if you groom the plants and give them food and water, but if you really want choice flowers for fall you had better be ready with another crop of seedlings. As a rule, it is the flowers from the late plantings that take the prizes in the fall shows.

Biennials and perennials, if planted early last month, should be fed now with a weak solution of liquid fertilizer. Chrysanthemums should be watched closely this month; continue feeding, spraying and watering when dry. Keep the side growths regularly removed from the exhibition types. The garden varieties and decorative types which produce small to medium-size flowers should be pinched again this month. Heavy pinching of these types induces stocky plants and more flower buds. (See Chapter 16.)

Small-flowered **chrysanthemums and dahlias** usually give a fair crop of bloom with very little attention, but if you are growing the exhibition types you had better keep right after them to see that they are kept in vigorous growth throughout summer and fall. A little fertilizer every two weeks and adequate moisture will usually do the job.

It may sound a bit like cheating, but you can deceive the very accommodating **rain lilies** (zephyranthes) and induce them to make a nice show of bloom by soaking the earth about their roots with the hose. The bulbs seem to think it is rain, and in three or four days the bloom spikes will begin to appear.

We have reports from several areas that **bulbous irises** (English, Dutch and Spanish) are disappearing after a season or two of bloom. It is our opinion that our very hot, dry summers cause the bulbs to deteriorate, and that if they are watered well occasionally during the dry periods there will be fewer losses. This treatment seems safer than digging and storing the bulbs.

We cannot urge too strongly that all **trees and shrubs** planted last season be given plenty of water during summer and late fall. Especially must the azaleas and camellias be watched; they may die quickly if they get too dry.

Most **perennial phlox** will give additional bloom if the faded flower heads are cut back and the old plants watered and fed. If the weather is dry, see that they do not suffer for water.

If the leaves of your fancy-leaf **caladiums** seem to be fading, although you have fed and watered them properly, let them rest for two or three weeks, then feed them well and apply plenty of water; you may be rewarded with a fresh crop of handsome new leaves.

PRUNING AND PROPAGATION

July through August is a good time to cut back the **wisterias** that are getting out of bounds, and pruning now seems to induce the setting of flower buds for next spring. Prune back tree wisterias several times during the season in order to induce better bloom and throw nourishment to the trunk and main branches. Few shrubs or trees are more colorful than a tree wisteria in spring, so, if you have no place for the heavy rambunctious vine, try the tree form.

The new **butterfly bushes** (buddleia), are dependable summer and fall bloomers. At this season remove much of the top growth —including all faded flowers—cultivate lightly, feed thoroughly and keep well watered for superior late-summer bloom.

Formal hedges should be given attention at frequent intervals. If clipped every week they will always look neat and attractive, and a heavy cutting will never be required.

Summer cuttings may still be taken of deciduous flowering shrubs and broad-leaf evergreens. Although some species may make no growth when taken so late, they should form roots or at least make a callus and be ready to make roots with the first breath of spring.

Garden pools should not be allowed to become overgrown with plants. And don't expect the fish in your pool to multiply satisfactorily unless they are fed. The best foods to use are the specially prepared ones found at the pet stores, but if you forget to buy it, do not let the fish go hungry; give them raw oatmeal and bread or cracker crumbs. Starved mother fish sometimes devour their young. Do not give more food than they will clean up in ten or fifteen minutes.

CONTROL OF PESTS AND DISEASE

August is a good month for using the chemical weed killers. There are many brands prepared for control of many different kinds of weeds, and some are very selective. Your dealer should be able to tell you what you need for the control of any particular weed. Be careful about getting these chemical killers on your flowers. Always use separate sprayers or sprinklers for the "killers." The minutest residue left in the sprayer can play havoc with your flowers when the sprayer is used again for spraying them. A friend lost a number of fine roses by spraying them with a sprayer that had been used for weed killers and had not been thoroughly cleaned.

If there are showers this month, you can expect your roses to develop **black spot** and the crape myrtles, phlox and zinnias to be attacked by **mildew**. There are many good fungicides available at your garden store; get one and make weekly applications until the trouble is under control.

Every year there is evidence of heavy infestation of **scale** on camellias throughout the South. If the leaves have yellowish splotches, examine the undersides for scale. If found, spray at once with a summer scale spray which may be obtained from the seed stores. Better not to spray while the temperature is above 90 degrees, however. Scale may soon kill valuable plants; better keep an eye on them.

In many cases, **aphids** that attack water lilies can be washed off with the hose and will give no further trouble. If you want to use a spray, pyrethrum is perhaps the safest one.

PLANTING LIST FOR AUGUST

Seeds

Balsam
  (Impatiens)
Calendula
Cockscomb
  (Celosia)
Cornflower
  (Centaurea)

Cosmos
English daisy
Hollyhock
Marigold
Mignonette
Periwinkle
  (*Vinca rosea*)

Portulaca
Texas bluebonnet
  (*Lupinus
  texensis*)
Tithonia
Torenia
Zinnia

Bulbs, Rhizomes and Tubers

*Amaryllis
  belladonna*
Billbergia
Colchicum
Daylily
  (Hemerocallis)
Habranthus

Iris
  German
  Japanese
  Louisiana
  I. cristata
  I. kaempferi
  I. unguicularis
Jacobaean lily
  (Sprekelia)

Madonna lily
  (Lilium
  candidum)
Rain lily
  (Zephyranthes)
Sternbergia
Wandflower
  (Sparaxis)

9

September

Get out your catalogs, especially the new ones, and check on the hardy annuals to be planted next month. After deciding on the seeds you will need, call your local seed store to see if they will have them in stock; if not, go ahead and place mail orders at once.

If seeds of the hardy annuals are planted during the thirty-day period from the middle of September to the middle of October, they will have time to develop root systems that will enable most of them to keep growing during the winter. By spring the young plants should be well developed, stocky and strong. Should you wait until late winter to plant, the seedlings will not have time to develop sufficient root systems, there will be more winter injury and you will have weak plants that will not bloom nearly so well or so long as those planted early. These suggestions apply to the Middle South (Zone 8). In the Upper South (Zone 7) planting may begin about a week or ten days earlier; in the Lower and Deep South (Zones 9 and 10), it comes a week or two later. If the seeds of hardy annuals can be obtained early enough to give them a few weeks of cool storage before planting, germination will be better.

Check the garden now for material to be potted and brought indoors later. See that the plants you intend to bring in the house get plenty of room to develop, and if a little pruning is needed to improve their appearance, do it while they are still growing in the garden.

This is a good time to take softwood cuttings of such plants as geraniums, fuchsias, heliotropes and lantanas. Cuttings taken now should give you strong, stocky plants for spring. It is especially important that you take geranium cuttings now to have strong plants for growing next spring.

If you grow Chinese hibiscus, you should be able to grow bougainvillea under approximately the same conditions. Many are grown in the Middle South in large pots and small tubs and can be moved indoors in winter. Staked and cut back to thirty or forty inches, they make lovely plants and will give abundant bloom. *B. glabra sanderiana* is not the prettiest but is considered the hardiest and is recommended for those areas where some protection must be given.

In the northern belt of the South, dig gladiolus planted in the spring if the leaves have turned brown; the spikes will soon disappear and the corms will be hard to locate. You may dig them after the leaves have turned brown, even though there is still some green in the flower stalks.

If there are rainy periods in September, it would be a good time to repair the lawn. Be sure to break up and enrich the area before planting seed or placing sprigs or sod. If you use centipede, St. Augustine or zoysia, and cannot get started soon, you had better wait until spring. Many of us lose much of the benefit of our winter rye grass by planting too late. Plant late this month or early next month so the grass will have time to become established before winter arrives. (See Chapter 23.)

Practically all of the weeds are trying to make seeds now, and this is a good time to pull them out before the seeds mature. Pulling one weed now may save pulling a thousand next spring.

This month the exhibition chrysanthemums will be putting out all manner of side shoots. Pinch off these shoots just as soon as they are long enough to handle. If left on the plants, they weaken the flower-producing canes and affect the quality of the blooms. (See Chapter 16.)

WHAT TO PLANT

In the southern margin of the Southeast, along the Gulf Coast and across Florida, this is the planting month for those things you depend on for winter bloom. In the Rio Grande Valley, in the area of New Orleans, Mobile, Pensacola and Tallahassee, and across to the east, you may plant **annuals** for winter bloom: calendulas, gaillardias, alyssum, sweet peas, myosotis, nasturtiums, nicotiana, petunias, poppies, snapdragons and verbena. It is this winter bloom that makes the South a distinctive "land of flowers." Let's make the most of our opportunities by planting heavily.

Check on volunteer plants. If September is a bit cloudy and wet, or if the beds have been adequately watered, you will probably find numerous seedlings by the last of the month in those areas where hardy annuals were grown: larkspur, poppies, California poppies, phlox and others. These self-sown seeds germinate early, make good growth, usually stand the winter well—and make good strong plants that will give superior bloom in the spring.

This is pansy planting month in the South, if we hope to have bloom for Christmas and New Year's Day. Buy the best seed you can find, locate the bed in a shady spot, but with good overhead light. For soil for the seedbed, use a blend of one part each of sand and peat moss and two parts garden loam. After running the mixture through a screen of hardware cloth, place it in the bed and wet lightly. Sow the seeds and cover them with a sprinkling of sand, then press them into the soil with a board. Finally, cover with newspaper, burlap or old cloth. Check the bed daily and remove covering with the first sign of germination.

In the Upper South (Zone 7) **spring-flowering bulbs** (except tulips and hyacinths) should be planted this month or next, just as soon as the bulbs are available. Thus the next sixty days are planting time for anemones and ranunculi, which are becoming more popular in the South each season.

October is considered the best month in most areas of the

South for planting daffodils; but if you can get the bulbs, there is certainly no objection to planting them in September. Soleil d'Or, Chinese sacred lilies and paper-whites planted now in the Middle South should be in bloom by late December. When we see daffodils blooming cheerfully in early spring, we always wish we had planted more of them. If you have the space, plant them by the dozens, hundreds or thousands—no danger of getting too many. Try clumps along the shrubbery borders and in the perennial beds. Be sure to try a few of the new kinds; plan now for a daffodil show next spring. We in the South are missing a big bet on daffodils. They offer so much for so little.

If you plan to move your amaryllis this year and failed to do the job right after they bloomed, now is a good time to take care of them. It's a good time to order and plant new bulbs, too.

Across from Tupelo to Birmingham and points east, place orders for Dutch iris and plant as soon as received. This iris is very pretty, is superior as a cutting flower and does well in most sections of the South. Now is also a good time to plant the winter-flowering *Iris unguicularis*. Once established, this iris will stand any amount of drought and bloom at midwinter. Mix a generous proportion of bone meal into the soil in planting.

You may plant callas, freesias, crocuses, grape hyacinths, ixias, wandflowers, watsonias and zephyranthes as soon as the bulbs are available. Callas planted now in the Middle South may come into bloom before cold weather arrives. Give them a deep rich soil and cover the roots three to four inches deep. Water lightly until growth begins, then water more liberally.

Some garden writers are telling their readers to plant "baby glads" in the fall, but I am not sure what a "baby" glad is. We have the standard kinds, the miniatures and the species *Gladiolus*. We have found through the years that the species glads should be planted in the South during the fall months—some of them will come into bloom in February and March—but, for the standard type, February is plenty early to plant in the Middle South, in our experience.

This is also a very good month for planting several species of irises, especially the bearded, Louisiana, Oriental and Siberian kinds. Keep well watered after planting. You may want to order the additional bearded irises you failed to order earlier, and to rework the beds and separate rhizomes of old plantings that were neglected earlier.

There are a number of **perennials** that should be divided and reset during September and October, particularly daisies, day-lilies, salvia and phlox. You may also make new plantings of these species.

It is easy to move chrysanthemums even after they have started blooming. Dug with a clump of earth at their roots, they may be potted for indoor bloom or transferred to vacant spots in the perennial border. Keep them well watered after they are moved, and they will hardly wilt at all.

Plan now for the fall **vegetable garden**; we can grow almost as many things in the South in the fall as in the spring. The ground should be prepared a little deeper, made a little richer, and the seed planted a little deeper than in the spring. Practically all leafy vegetables and many of the root crops may be planted in the fall. If you can find them, try putting out plants of collards, tomatoes, cabbage and onions. Let's do our part by growing every ounce of food possible.

PRUNING, FEEDING, WATERING

Fall-blooming **roses** need a little special attention this month. Whether you gave them a rest during midsummer or not, prune them lightly now, thinning out some of the excess interior wood and feed them. Unless you live in the Lower South, this will be their last feeding of the season. (In Florida and the Rio Grande Valley roses can be fed a little later.) A heaping tablespoonful of plant food for each plant, or two pounds (6–8–8) to each hundred square feet of bed, is about right. Remove all dead flower heads, cut back the blind canes (those without growing terminal buds) and, unless there is ample rain, soak the beds well. (See Chapter 22.)

The development of seeds is an exhaustive phase in the life of a plant. If you want your **annuals and perennials** to continue growing and blooming, keep all faded flowers clipped and let none go to seed. A light shearing, with a little cultivation, feeding and watering, will do wonders for growth and bloom. (If some, like petunias, are getting leggy, prune them back.) This also applies to roses, on which the formation of hips or seed pods saps much of the vitality of the plants. Snip off all faded flowers; the garden will not only look neater but the plants will show more vigor.

Seedlings of perennials, especially irises and daylilies, will be happier with an occasional feeding of liquid plant food. If you use a special food, be sure to follow the directions carefully.

September is many times a very dry month, and **large shrubs and trees** planted last season should be closely watched. One of the plastic soil soakers is perhaps the best thing you can find for watering them. Circle it around the specimen and let it run for several hours if necessary to get the soil wet down to the roots of the plants.

Azaleas and camellias are now busy growing flower buds for the coming season. If you want good bloom, see that the plants get plenty of water during the fall months. Better check on the mulches also and renew any that have deteriorated too much.

In addition to the azaleas and camellias, many of the early **spring-flowering shrubs,** as well, form their flower buds in late summer and fall, and ample moisture at this season is important. Dry weather during the fall months can result in faulty centers in the flower buds, causing them to drop off instead of opening when blooming time arrives.

CONTROL OF PESTS

If your canna leaves do not unfold promptly, they probably have **canna leaf rollers.** Slit the roll with a sharp blade and you will find the little green worms that are causing the trouble. Destroy the worms and spray with a reliable insecticide.

During the cool nights in September, **aphids** seem to multiply miraculously. They come in a variety of colors (red, green and

black are the most common), and the tender growths on chrysanthemums, roses and spireas are their favorite feeding places. A
reliable insecticide spray will stop them, but two or three applications may be necessary. Every pest that isn't killed crawls
over to another spot and starts a new family.

PLANTING LIST FOR SEPTEMBER

Seeds

Alyssum
Arctotis
Baby blue-eyes
 (Nemophila)
Baby's-breath
 (Gypsophila)
Calendula
California poppy
 (Eschscholtzia)
Calliopsis
Candytuft (Iberis)
Carnation
 (Dianthus)
Chinese
 forget-me-not
 (Cynoglossum)
Coreopsis, perennial

Cornflower
 (Centaurea)
Daisy
 English
 Shasta
Forget-me-not
 (Myosotis)
Gaillardia
Gerbera
Hollyhock
Lobelia
Lupine
Mignonette
Nasturtium
Nicotiana
Pansy
Petunia

Phlox, annual
Poppy
 Iceland
 Shirley
Queen Anne's lace
Scabiosa
Snapdragon
Statice
Stock
Sweet pea, early
Sweet William
Verbena
Viola odorata
Wallflower
 (Cheiranthus)

Bulbs, Rhizomes and Tubers

Amaryllis
Anemone
Calla lily
 (Zantedeschia)
Chinese sacred lily
 (*Narcissus tazetta
 orientalis*)
Crocus
Daffodils (Narcissi)
 in variety
Daylily
 (Hemerocallis)
Freesia

Gladiolus
Iris
 Bearded
 Dutch
 Japanese
 Louisiana
 Oriental
 Siberian
 I. unguicularis
Ixia
Lily-of-the-valley
 (Convallaria)

Lily
 Madonna
 Regal
Montbretia
Oxalis
Rain lily
 (Zephyranthes)
Ranunculus
Wandflower
 (Sparaxis)
Watsonia

10

October

Throughout most of the South, October is the month for planning and planting our spring gardens. Almost all the success and beauty of our gardens in March, April and May depends on what we plan and plant in October.

If your shrubs, evergreens and climbing roses are outgrowing their space, you can cut them back lightly without any damage, but wait until late winter for the heavy pruning.

Before you start fall planting, give your flower beds a thorough cleaning. There are usually a number of spent annuals, some matured perennials and a few weeds that need clearing out. A good cleaning now will destroy many weed seeds, insect eggs and young.

Leaves will be falling late this month. Don't burn them; they make excellent leaf mold, and most of our soils need much of it. A friend has a small net which he keeps handy to skim off the leaves from the lily pool before they become water-soaked and sink. A few leaves in the pool may do no harm, but too many will decay and foul the water.

This is the time for potting geraniums, chrysanthemums, begonias and other things for bringing indoors for winter bloom. Pot up, water well and leave in the shade for several days before frost forces you to bring them indoors. They will do better than if brought in freshly potted. You may find volunteer plants of marigolds, zinnias, torenias, petunias and other species just waiting to be potted and brought in to brighten the interior. Try to dig with a solid ball of earth at the roots, and keep well watered.

Early this month is also a good time to take cuttings of Chinese hibiscus, acalyphas and crotons and root in a sunny window, greenhouse or heated garage.

In many areas, this is the month for digging fancy-leaf caladiums. Information released from the Florida Experiment Station confirms my belief that in many cases the cause of winter rot is that the corms are stored with too much moisture or are allowed to get too cold. When the leaves begin to die in the fall, dig and let them dry in the shade for a week or ten days, then clean them and let them dry in the sun for another ten days. If there has been much rain just prior to digging, a longer period of curing may be necessary. (Commercially, they are dried in kilns, using artificial heat.) A garden neighbor stores hers (and she grows hundreds of them) in a closet where the temperature is about 70 degrees, constant, throughout the winter. Not only is this necessary to keep the corms from freezing, but they should be given a comparatively warm storage; any temperature below 50 degrees is not good for them.

If it has not yet been done, now is the time to dig gladiolus corms.

For light forcing, pot up choice bulbs of daffodils, hyacinths, tulips and Dutch irises, bury the pots outdoors in a sunny spot and begin bringing them indoors after six to eight weeks. Their forcing requires but little effort and you will enjoy their winter bloom.

In the Middle South (Zone 8), paper-white narcissus may bloom outdoors by the last of December if the weather is mild, but they are easily forced indoors, in pebbles and water, and may be timed for continuous bloom.

If your community is having a spring-flowering bulb show, now is the time to do your planting for it. If you are not planning a regular show, you may convert your own garden into one by

just a little planning and effort. The spring-flowering bulbs give
us a great show for the money. We can hardly beat them.

Every year when digging up the flower beds, we cut into some
bulbs because they do not have their location properly marked.
We suggest you mark all spots where bulbs, peonies and other
things that lose their tops in winter are grown. It is easy to forget
precisely where they grew.

WHAT TO PLANT

While the planting may properly begin in September, October
is the main month for planting **spring-flowering bulbs** in most of
the South. With the exception of hyacinths and tulips, all of the
spring-flowering bulbs, both "major" and "minor" ones, can and
should be planted now. In the Middle South (Zone 8) order your
tulip and hyacinth bulbs and, when the bulbs arrive, place them
in the refrigerator to remain until planting time, about the first
of December. In the Upper South (Zone 7) they may be planted
in late October or November.

First position the bulbs in their proper places on top of the
soil and plant each one at the proper depth for that particular
species. A trowel comes in handy for this work. Be sure the holes
are wide enough at the bottom for the bulbs to rest firmly without air space beneath. The earth should be firmed around each
bulb and the entire planting watered when it is completed.

When as many as a dozen bulbs are to be planted in one location, as in a bed, remove all soil to the proper depth, break up
the soil below, set the bulbs all in place on the same level and
cover with the removed soil.

Many good gardeners think that daffodils, hyacinths and tulips
should be planted at least six inches deep. If you are trying to
save your tulip bulbs for another season, you had better plant
them eight to twelve inches deep; if they are treated as an annual
crop, six inches would be all right.

In the Upper South, all daffodils are supposed to do well, but
here in the Middle South we have found that while practically

all the small- to medium-flowered daffodils do well, many of the giant-flowered types do not flower well after the first year.

Down in the Deep South the giant double hyacinths do not seem to thrive and may not come back after the first year. After the foliage has matured, try digging and storing them in a cool spot for the summer. In some of these warmer areas I understand the small "Roman" hyacinths are generally successful. Here in Meridian we never dig the small kinds, and they always come back and bloom strongly. The large-flowered kinds usually play out after two or three seasons.

In addition to daffodils, there are many other bulbs and bulbous things that can be planted now, including amaryllis, anemone, billbergia, calla, camassia, daylily, freesia, lilies of various kinds, liriope, ornithogalum, ranunculus, watsonia and zephyranthes.

There are a number of small or minor bulbs—chionodoxa, grape hyacinth, scilla, snowdrop, snowflake—that will brighten up the garden beds in early spring. Ixia is one of the prettiest of them, but one rarely sees it in Southern gardens. These minor bulbs may not always come back 100 percent, but the ones that do will pay off well. From a dozen scillas planted several years ago, only one came back, but it soon grew into a large clump, and after dividing we now have a sizable bed.

All forms of **bulbous irises**—English, Dutch and Spanish—may be planted this month or next. Dutch irises are becoming more and more important in Southern gardens. They can be planted any time during October and November. Even early December is not too late, although late plantings bloom much later than early ones. The very early blue Wedgwood, planted with yellow pansies in front, always gives a lovely effect. Imperator, which blooms later than Wedgwood, is one of the best yellows. Other desirable varieties are Golden Harvest, White Excelsior, Bronze Beauty and White Superior.

For the all-white spot in your garden, plant white irises, white crocuses, white tulips, white daffodils, perennial candytuft, white pentstemon, regal lilies and white azaleas.

Camellia sasanqua is coming into bloom this month, and it is a good time to plant it. Visit the nurseries and sales yards and check the varieties in bloom, and you will be able to get the colors and bloom forms you like best.

You may continue planting both **daylilies and Shasta daisies** through this month, but I'd get the job finished just as soon as possible. Although these perennials will tolerate considerable drought, both will need adequate moisture right after planting. Even if the soil is moist, water well after planting; if the weather is dry, water copiously and see that the plants get plenty of moisture until they are established.

If **rye grass** is to be planted for a winter lawn, do it this month. While covering with sand or soil gives much better germination, it is not essential. Clip the lawn closely, sow the seeds which have been mixed with fertilizer, and wet down; then water occasionally until the young grass gets started. More watering is necessary where the seed is not covered, as there is danger of the seedlings dying after germination unless there is ample moisture.

In the Rio Grande Valley, along the Gulf Coast and in most sections of Florida (Zone 9), you may now plant many of the **summer annuals** for winter bloom. Through the Middle South (Zone 8) and the Upper South (Zone 7), you may plant the hardy annuals for spring bloom. February is another month for planting these hardy annuals, but fall planting is much better.

In most sections of the South hardy annuals should be planted in late September or in October. They are also planted in the fall in the cooler areas, but for different reasons. When planted in the fall in the North the seeds do not germinate until spring, and the fall planting serves as a kind of stratification, resulting in better germination.

Down here, our seeds germinate within a few weeks after planting and give us strong, stocky plants before winter arrives. Many of them are winter-hardy and with the coming of spring the root systems are strong, the growth rapid and the bloom early and profuse. We will get much stronger plants and longer and better bloom from hardy annuals planted in the fall. Hard freezes may get some of them, but the chance is well worth taking.

In the event you fail to get your hardy annuals planted by the end of October, there is no advantage, as I see it, to planting in midwinter; wait until February. The species classified as "hardy" include alyssum, California poppy, calliopsis, annual poppy, larkspur, annual phlox, pansy, English daisy, cornflower, calendula and a few others.

Seeds of hardy annuals planted this month will give winter bloom in the Rio Grande Valley, along the Gulf Coast and in Florida; farther north they will form strong, stocky plants for early spring bloom. In this group of plants are ageratum, alyssum, anchusa, calendula, California poppy, marigold, nasturtium, petunia, phlox, Queen Anne's lace, snapdragon, stock, sweet pea, Sweet William, and zinnia.

Preparation for fall planting involves a bit more care than spring work. Spade the bed a little deeper, use just a little more plant food, and cover the seed with a little more soil than in the spring. If the weather is dry—and it probably will be—wet the beds down thoroughly, all the way down, and let them settle for a few days before planting the seeds.

Late this month and through November is an ideal time to set out strong established plants of **biennials** for next spring's bloom. It is now too late to plant seed of biennials, but if you can find strong, stocky plants and set them out soon, they should give good bloom in the spring.

Make another planting of English daisies and pansies. Pansy plants are available at the garden stores this month. You will usually find the plants well started, stocky and strong, and some of them already in flower bud. Planted late this month they will have a head start over your home-grown seedlings. Pansies are much more effective when planted in mass by colors.

For years I tried to determine the better season (spring or fall) for dividing **perennials** and long ago reached the conclusion that, for most species, fall is preferable. The period from the middle of September to the last of October is perhaps the best. This early dividing and transplanting give time for the plants to become established and make some growth before hard cold arrives. Not all perennials should be divided and reset every season, but for those that must be divided, fall is usually better than spring. When division and replanting are done in the fall, make sure the newly set plants are kept well watered.

September and early October are good months for planting **vegetables** for the home table. Earlier in the Upper South, and a bit later in the Deep South, you may plant beets, broccoli, Brussels sprouts, carrots, endive, mustard, turnips and Swiss chard.

FEEDING AND WATERING

The weather is something about which none of us can tell very much, but October is many times very dry, especially in the Middle and Deep South. Remember, many **shrubs** form their spring-flowering buds in the late summer and fall and must have adequate moisture for proper bud development.

Along the coast, feed the early **sweet peas** that you planted in August and September for winter bloom. Use a heaping table-spoonful of balanced plant food to a gallon of water and apply liberally every two weeks. Many gardeners prefer waiting until November to plant the spring crop of flowers.

This is a vital period for **chrysanthemums**. Give them an application of liquid plant food—two tablespoonfuls to a gallon of water—every two weeks. Then, when color begins to show in the buds, discontinue feedings. Check the large-flowering or exhibition type for side shoots. (See Chapter 16.)

CONTROL OF PESTS AND DISEASE

In Zones 7 and 8, no more fertilizer should be given the roses this season; winter is too close. Feeding too late will encourage new growth which will be killed by the coming freezes. But you should continue spraying for **black spot**. Most winterkilling is caused by dieback, because the plant goes into winter without adequate foliage. A rose plant clothed with good foliage rarely suffers from dieback; it is the weak, little-foliaged plants that suffer. October is too early to plant bare-root roses in the Middle South. (See Chapter 22.)

If you have not already given them attention this fall, check all your plum trees and both ornamental and fruiting peach trees for **borers,** the evidence of which is a gum which oozes out of the bark of the trunk down near the ground. Whether evidence of borers is found or not, the trees should be treated in the fall. Mix your insecticide about double the strength for ordinary use and spray the trunk of the trees up for about two feet from the soil level. But before spraying, take a screwdriver or knife and clean out all the gum so that the spray can reach the damaged areas. In applying this "medicine," the most vital area is right where the trunk reaches the ground surface.

If you failed to spray your camellias last month, be sure to attend to that job at once. Talk to your garden store man about the new types of spray now being used in your area. Fall is also a good time to spray azaleas for **lace bugs.**

In the Rio Grande Valley and in Florida, spray gladiolus with insecticide to check **thrips,** the principal insect enemy of these flowers.

PLANTING LIST FOR OCTOBER

Seeds

Ageratum
Alyssum
Anchusa
Calendula
California poppy
  (Eschscholtzia)
Calliopsis
Candytuft (Iberis)
Carnation
  (Dianthus)

Chinese
  forget-me-not
  (Cynoglossum)
Cornflower
  (Centaurea)
Daisy
  *English
  Shasta
Hollyhock
Larkspur
Lupine
Pansy

Petunia
Phlox, annual
Poppy, Shirley
Queen Anne's lace
Snapdragon
  (Antirrhinum)
Stock
Sweet pea, early
Sweet William
Verbena
Viola odorata

Bulbs, Rhizomes and Tubers

Allium
Amaryllis
Anemone
Billbergia
Calla lily
  (Zantedeschia)
Camassia
Chionodoxa
Clivia
Daffodils (Narcissi)
  in variety
Daylily
  (Hemerocallis)
Freesia
Grape hyacinth
  (Muscari)

Iris
  Bearded
  Dutch
  Louisiana
  Siberian
  I. kaempferi
  I. spuria
  I. unguicularis
Ixia
Lily
  Easter
  Regal
  Tiger
  L. candidum
  L. centifolium
  L. speciosum
Liriope

Marica
Ornithogalum
Oxalis
Rain lily
  (Zephyranthes)
Ranunculus
Red-hot poker
  (Kniphofia)
Scilla
Snowdrop
  (Galanthus)
Snowflake
  (Leucojum)
Wandflower
  (Sparaxis)
Watsonia

---

* Plant in protected beds.

11

November

In all areas of the Upper South (Zone 7) you may begin planting in earnest this month such things as bare-root roses and shrubs, perennial vines and young trees, both ornamental and shade. All types of evergreens—broad-leaf and narrow-leaf—may be planted now. Shrubs, roses and trees planted this month will begin making root growth during the warm periods of winter and will be firmly established by the time spring arrives. It is especially important that larger specimens such as small-size trees be planted early so they will have a longer period to become established.

In the Middle South (Zone 8) you may begin planting such material as shrubs and roses about the middle of the month; and in the Lower South (Zone 9), about Thanksgiving.

Don't be in a hurry to do your winter pruning; there is still lots of time. In the Middle South the month of February is a good time for this work. Too early cutting stimulates premature growth that will be winterkilled by late freezes.

If you consider yourself a good gardener you will want to clean and oil all spades, sharpshooters, shovels, hoes and other garden tools before putting them away for the winter. Many of us here in the South use most of our garden tools so consistently and continuously that there is hardly a rest period for them. In this case, try to attend to each particular one during the slack time when it is not being used.

In the Upper South many of our green plants will either lose their leaves or be blighted by winter freezes, and a little window garden will do much to brighten the interiors. Your planning should really start in October, when plants in bud and bloom should be selected. You will find many things in your own garden that may be used: dwarf petunias, alyssums, tiny evergreens, divisions of asparagus ferns and little century plants.

You may wish to visit the dime stores, garden stores and florists' shops for dainty little containers for very small plants. While most of the plant material will not require full sun, an east or south window will normally be best.

In bringing the house plants indoors, handle them carefully so that they will get as little shock as possible. Place them on the porch or in a cool room for the first week or two. Bringing them from the outdoors directly into an overheated room spells trouble. Too much chill, however, will cause some of them—especially the poinsettias—to lose their leaves.

Dwarf tulips are among the most colorful of all house plants. For forcing, they should be potted right away, after being first chilled in the refrigerator for three or four weeks. A favorite potting soil is made by mixing equal parts of garden loam, sand and peat moss.

Pot some of the late chrysanthemums and bring them indoors. Placed in a sunny window, they will give you flowers for many weeks; some will go on blooming practically all winter. Also pot some of the petunias, marigolds, zinnias and other annuals now in bloom.

WHAT TO PLANT

How soon can planting of shrubs, roses and trees begin? The time varies with the latitude, of course, but a good guide is the falling of leaves from the deciduous shrubs and trees. When the leaves begin to fall heavily—usually November in the Middle South—it is safe to begin planting.

There is no better way to attract birds to the home grounds

than to grow an abundance of **fruiting shrubs** which will provide food for them. In ordering and selecting shrubs for the home grounds, do not overlook those that bear fruits. In addition to producing food for the birds, they add much color and appeal to the grounds in winter. During the months when there are few flowers and shrubs in bloom, the fruiting species will do much to supply needed color with their colorful fruit. Except in Zone 9, flowers are usually at a low level in midwinter, and it is then that the fruits of the shrubs show up to best advantage. Among the good fruiting shrubs are the several hollies, nandina, honeysuckle, elaeagnus, coralberry, snowberry, cotoneaster, pyracantha, and of course the privets (ligustrums), French mulberry, beautyberry, chokeberry and native hawthorns. Many of these fruits hang on all winter unless they are eaten by the birds.

If you can find space in your shrub plantings for such **winter-flowering shrubs** as camellia, eleagnus, *Viburnum tinus,* witchhazel, corylopsis and sweet olive, they will add much color and fragrance to the garden in midwinter. In the Middle South, *Jasminum nudiflorum,* winter honeysuckle and most of the Japanese quinces will be making much bloom by late December if the weather is normal.

The **Sasanqua camellias** should be in bloom now. They are unsurpassed as fall-flowering shrubs. If practical, visit a nursery and see them in bloom and make selections. You'll like this shrub, which can be transplanted while it is in full bloom.

Many of us will be planting **roses** this season. Each particular area has its favorite season for planting, but in most sections of the South the season is very long, and planting of bare-root plants may be done any time from November until late February or early March. Here in the Meridian area, which we consider Middle South, we think November and December are ideal months for planting, for the average winter. In the Upper South some gardeners report that, when planted in November or early December, the plants are sometimes killed back by winter freezes, and suggest planting in late January or February. Of course, if we knew in which month we would get our coldest weather, that information would influence our time of planting, but this we cannot know. (See Chapter 22.)

In looking around for **dwarf evergreens** to plant this month, do not fail to check on the many dwarf forms of holly now available. There are also some very pretty dwarf pyracanthas that are now in great demand.

If you are planning to move young **trees** from the open woods to your property, it's a good idea to root prune them and let them remain in their present locations for another season if practicable. Root pruning is accomplished by inserting the spade to the approximate depth of the blade in the soil, around the plant in a circle about twelve to twenty inches from the trunk, the distance from the trunk to be determined by the size of the tree to be moved. The spade should be withdrawn after each insertion without removing the earth. This induces the growth of many new feed roots up near the trunk, and these can be saved when the tree is dug. Most nurseries regularly root prune their young trees, thus producing a much better root system than is found on specimens brought in from the woods.

All evergreens of more than a few feet in height and all larger deciduous trees should be staked or given other support when planted, to prevent their being blown about by the wind. Use cloth strips, rubber or plastic hose or heavily insulated wire to fasten the plants at the support.

Give old flower beds a thorough cleaning before you begin planting anything in them. Remove all spent flowers and weeds. Sprinkling the beds with a suitable pesticide will destroy many insects wintering in the soil, and spraying with a reliable fungicide will tend to check fungi left by diseased plants.

There is still time to plant such **bulbs** as lilies (except the Madonna), daffodils, Dutch irises and minor bulbs like scillas, snowdrops, snowflakes, ranunculi and anemones. Around Houston, New Orleans, Tallahassee and across Florida you can also plant agapanthuses, callas, freesias and ornithogalums.

In the Upper South, you can plant tulips late this month; in the Middle South, you'll get better results if you postpone planting until the first of December. (See Chapter 21.)

It is not too late to plant **peonies** in the Upper South, but the job should be finished at once. Generally speaking, the single and Japanese varieties do better in the South.

Daylilies planted in the fall start root growth immediately, and the evergreen ones will make some top growth in early winter. Fall and early winter planting will result in much stronger plants and better bloom than can be expected from spring-planted ones. Old clumps can be divided now and reset. And don't forget to order some of the newer kinds. There is now a nationwide society for those who love and grow this flower.

In the Lower South, or citrus belt, **annuals** of all sorts can be planted now for late winter bloom. In the Middle South the hardy sorts can be planted early this month, but not later; the job must be finished at once or postponed until February. In this hardy group are such dependables as alyssum, calendula, California poppy, calliopsis, Chinese forget-me-not, gaillardia, larkspur, phlox, all kinds of poppies, and sweet peas. Sweet peas require very little attention after planting, and few annuals give lovelier color or more delightful fragrance. Early this month is the time for planting the main crop. Dig a trench about a foot deep and equally wide; fill in two thirds full of enriched soil, using some leaf mold or peat moss; add an inch or two of unfertilized soil and then plant the seeds. Fill the trench in the process of cultivation.

Through the Rio Grande Valley and around New Orleans, Pensacola and to the east, we can make a second planting of hardy annuals for early spring bloom. The more we plant now, the more bloom we will have in February, March and April.

In many parts of the South a number of **vegetables** can be planted this month. South of Marshall, Shreveport, Vicksburg and Montgomery, try carrots, kohlrabi, lettuce, turnips, mustard, tendergreens and onions. It is possible that they will not thrive, but the chance of success is worth the effort.

PLANT PROPAGATION

In all Southern areas you may begin taking **hardwood cuttings** of deciduous shrubs and evergreens. Do not make them too long—four or five inches will be plenty long, regardless of what the "book" says. (See Chapter 25.)

Nandinas are easily grown from seed. You may normally leave the seed on the plants until after the holidays, if you prefer, then gather and stratify them by placing alternate layers of seed and sand in a wooden box which should be left outdoors. In the spring, mash off the fleshy parts of the seed and plant them in a partially shady spot, covering with about a half inch of sandy soil. If you will check your old nandina plants before applying new mulches, you will probably find a number of seedlings under them. If taken up carefully and placed in a growing bed they will soon make nice bushy plants.

Dogwood seeds also are easily germinated if handled as suggested for nandinas.

There is still time to take cuttings of **geraniums** for spring-blooming plants. Cuttings taken now, given sufficient warmth and food, may even bloom in late winter. Water occasionally with an iron-sulphate solution, one heaping tablespoonful to a gallon of water.

PLANT NUTRITION

The **leaves** are falling now on practically every homesite in the South. Let them go back into the soil as humus, for if we take nutrients from the soil in the form of foliage, fruit and flowers and give nothing back, it will soon be bankrupt, depleted and lifeless. Pile the excess leaves and let them decay for use next spring. Many of them can be used to great advantage as mulches. Oak leaves, for example, applied directly, make a good mulch for many shrubs and young trees. (Straw and pine needles are better, however, for small plants like perennials.)

In cases where the lawn is thin and the leaves do not tend to smother the grass, a small quantity of leaves shredded with the lawn mower and left on the sod will be beneficial. If, however, there is sufficient quantity to kill the grass they should be removed.

If you failed to plant rye grass earlier, there is still time. If an early planting turns yellow, the grass probably needs more plant food.

Watch the seedbeds this month, especially the irises, daylilies and perennials, and see that they get plenty of moisture. If you have English daisies, pansies or other semihardy things still in these beds, they will probably appreciate a little food in the form of liquid fertilizer. Pansies, particularly, like lots of plant food and should be fed normally at intervals of two to four weeks. All prepared plant foods should be used, of course, according to directions.

Seedlings left too long in the seedbeds, especially English daisies and pansies, will soon run up and become leggy. Avoid this by lifting the little seedlings, with a bit of the soil to their roots, and transferring either to a growing bed or their permanent places. Do not let them crowd.

Buds will soon begin showing on the early varieties of camellias, and the plants will need plenty of moisture at their roots. If the weather is dry soak them at least once each week. This also applies to many of the azaleas.

CONTROL OF SCALE

Look over the camellias for the various scales to which they are susceptible. If the insects are found, take a soft cloth and lukewarm, soapy water and wash the infested leaves. Oil sprays are the standard remedy, but they are not safe to use on evergreen plants when there is danger of freezing or when the temperature is above 90 degrees. They may be applied in early spring after the danger of low temperatures is past. However, you may apply a dormant spray to flowering almonds, flowering peaches, lilacs, dogwoods and other deciduous shrubs and trees that are subject to attack by scale.

PLANTING LIST FOR NOVEMBER

Seeds

*Ageratum
Alyssum
Anchusa
Baby blue-eyes
(Nemophila)
California poppy
(Eschscholtzia)
Calendula
Calliopsis
Candytuft (Iberis)
Carnation
(Dianthus)

Chinese
forget-me-not
(Cynoglossum)
Cornflower
(Centaurea)
*English daisy
Larkspur
Lupine
Nierembergia
*Pansy
Petunia

Phlox, annual
Poppy, Shirley
Queen Anne's lace
Snapdragon
(Antirrhinum)
Stock
Sweet pea
Sweet William
Verbena
Viola odorata

Bulbs, Rhizomes and Tubers

Alstroemeria
Amaryllis
Anemone
Billbergia
Calla lily
(Zantedeschia)
Camassia
Clivia (in pots)
Crinum
Daffodil
(Narcissus)
Daylily
(Hemerocallis)
Freesia
Grape hyacinth
(Muscari)
Hyacinth

Iris
Dutch
Louisiana
Siberian
I. kaempferi
I. spuria
I. unguicularis
Ismene
Ixia
Liatris
Lily
Easter
Regal
Tiger
L. candidum
L. speciosum
Liriope

Ornithogalum
Oxalis
Rain lily
(Zephyranthes)
Ranunculus
Red-hot poker
(Kniphofia)
Scilla
Snowdrop
(Galanthus)
Snowflake
(Leucojum)
Spider lily
(Hymenocallis)
Wandflower
(Sparaxis)
Watsoni⸱

---

* Plant in protected beds.

12

December

Compared with the rest of the year, December is a dull gardening month in most sections of the South, but there is certainly enough work to keep us busy after we take time out for the holidays and holiday activities. Many species, especially the shrubby things, can be planted now. Our winters are short, and unless we plant early there will not be time enough for the plants to become established before the warm spring days arrive. Root growth should be firmly established before leaf growth begins.

The beauty of our native evergreens is evident every day in the year but never more so than in December, when the leaves have fallen from the many deciduous species and their branches and twigs are left bare. It is now that we can appreciate the evergreens to the fullest of their beauty. And the season for planting evergreens in the South is a long one; right now—December—is a very good time, especially for the pines.

Giving living Christmas trees as holiday gifts is gaining force in many sections of the South. This is a fine custom, but you must be selective in your purchases. Be sure there is a place on the recipient's grounds for the particular type of tree you have in mind, and that it is of a species that will thrive in his location. The thought is not new, but for a garden friend nothing can be more fitting than a good garden book or a subscription to a good garden magazine. A magazine or book may be a gentle reminder of your thoughtfulness all the years ahead, and it is something that will be of practical use.

Next to planting shrubby things, perhaps the most important garden activity for December is rooting hardwood or winter cuttings (see Chapter 25). If you failed to take all the hardwood cuttings last month that you will want this year, you may finish up this month. Almost all of us regret each season that we did not take more cuttings the season before. We always need more plants to fill in; and nothing makes more suitable gifts for friends than little plants we have rooted ourselves. You may take cuttings not only of the deciduous things but of many of the broad-leaf evergreens as well. Taken this late, not all will root, but most of them should.

WHAT TO PLANT

Continue planting all sorts of shrubs, roses, perennial vines and trees this month. January and February are sometimes very wet months, and you may find the ground too wet to plant on most of the days that would otherwise be favorable. So it is an act of smartness to get our winter planting behind us as soon as we can. With few exceptions, all shrubby things and trees should be planted early, and most certainly before the leaf buds begin to swell. If you wait, you will find yourself running into warm spring weather—and that would be bad.

Sawdust is a wonderful soil conditioner if used properly. I use a full shovelful in the soil under and around each plant when planting or transplanting perennials; for shrubs, from two to three times as much is used, depending on the size. Oak and cypress sawdust mixed with the soil is fine for azaleas, gardenias, camellias and other acid-loving plants. Pine sawdust should be at least a year old before being used and should be mixed well with the soil.

My many years of experience in gardening convince me that

improper planting causes more trouble with shrubs, roses and trees than anything else. The main trouble is in failure to dig the hole deep enough and big enough. There should be room in the bottom for several inches of prepared soil, containing a liberal quantity of leaf mold or peat moss, before the plant is placed, and for several inches of the soil mixture between the roots and the walls of the hole.

December is the best month of the year to plant **trees** in the South. Early planting is important, and the larger the specimen the earlier it should be planted. You may get by with planting small items as late as February, but the larger sizes definitely should be planted now so they can become established by spring.

In selecting trees for your grounds, do not overlook those that give brilliant color in the fall. The Chinese tallow trees, maples, sour woods, black gums, sweet gums, beeches, dogwoods and several species of oaks seem to vie with each other to see which can put on the most brilliant display of fall color. Of all our long planting season, December is the best month to plant trees in most areas.

Contrary to the general impression, pines grow very fast in good soil and with a moderate amount of moisture. On the lawn area, where they get the benefit of plant food and water applied to the grass, they may grow twice as fast as those planted in the woodland areas. One-year seedlings can be had at a moderate cost and will live almost 100 percent if properly handled. After the first year they will need practically no attention. However, one may gain several years in growth by obtaining plants already started in containers.

The proper depth of planting is most important. If too shallow, the roots dry out and are burned by the sun; if too deep, sufficient air does not reach the roots, and many plants may attempt to put out a new set of root systems just under the surface. If you get the plant the exact depth it grew in the nursery you will hardly go wrong. You may set strong plants about an inch deeper than they grew, but that should be the limit.

If the tree is large enough to be swayed in the wind, stake it;

but never bank earth up around the trunk of a shrub or tree. Rather, leave a slight depression around the plant to catch and hold water.

On-the-spot recommendations for planting **roses** vary slightly in the different sections of the South, but almost everywhere the accepted season includes December, January and February. Personally, I am an advocate of early planting unless there are local conditions which militate against it; my favorite month is December. (See Chapter 22.)

When moved with soil at their roots, as they usually are, **azaleas** and **camellias** can be easily handled when they are in full bloom. Planting when in bloom enables the purchaser to see exactly what he is getting. But earlier planting has many advantages too. It enables the plant to put on new roots and become firmly established before the warm weather of spring arrives.

There are very few **annuals** that can be planted in the Upper South this month; September, October and until about the middle of November is the best time for planting hardy annuals, and it is hardly worthwhile to plant during December and January. If not yet planted, let's wait until February.

In the Rio Grande Valley, along the Gulf Coast and in most of Florida, however, December is a good time to plant alyssum, calendula, candytuft, carnation, calliopsis, cornflower, English daisy, feverfew, gaillardia, larkspur, nierembergia, pansy, phlox, snapdragon, stock, strawflower, sweet pea, Sweet William and verbena. In the same area, clip faded flowers from early planted annuals, cultivate them lightly and give them a liberal feeding of balanced plant food.

Check the English daisies and pansies, and transplant them before they begin to crowd. Lift with small clumps of soil at the roots, transplant immediately and the plants will experience no shock whatever. Fed well, the early plantings should give you bloom for Christmas.

You may continue to plant daffodils and the other minor bulbs if you can find firm, solid bulbs, but if they become soft they will hardly be worth planting. While most **spring-flowering bulbs** (except tulips) should have been planted earlier, December is not too late, but be sure to finish up this planting before the month ends. Most of us could make our early spring garden more colorful by using more of the little bulbs like chionodoxa, fritillaria, grape hyacinth and scilla. Do not wait longer to plant.

Tulips and hyacinths which have been chilled in the refrigerator for several weeks may now be planted, but do this planting early in the month.

In the Rio Grande Valley, along the Gulf Coast and in most of Florida (Zone 9) you may plant such bulbous things as agapanthus, amaryllis, daffodils, hyacinths, Dutch irises and practically all the lilies except the Madonna, if you can get sound, firm bulbs. At this late season it would probably be well to soak the bulbs in water overnight before planting.

OTHER OUTDOOR ACTIVITIES

Freezing is a drying process; while it may seem unreasonable, plants lacking in moisture suffer from freezes much more than those that have adequate moisture, If there is not ample rainfall in your section, carry artificial watering right on through the winter.

It is better not to feed shrubs and trees in winter; just place a good mulch around them. Early feeding, like early pruning, tends to stimulate too early growth. Delay feeding until about the time the leaf buds begin to swell in February or early March. But mulches are all-important. Check to see that everything that should have a mulch has a good one. For small growing things straw is much better than leaves, but for trees and most medium-to-large-size shrubs leaves will usually make a good mulch.

Young azaleas and camellias will need some protection in the Upper South (Zone 7). A thick mulch of straw is excellent for this purpose, but old hay will do very well also. It is assumed, of course, that all established plants have already been adequately mulched.

Roses as a rule will need no protection from freezing during a normal winter in the Middle or Lower South (Zones 8 and 9), but in the Upper South earth should be piled up around the plants. This protection may not be necessary for mild winters, but when a very severe cold comes it is needed.

Hardy water lilies should need no protection during normal winters in the South; neither do the goldfish in the pool, assuming the pool is kept well filled with water. (Should the pool freeze over for more than a few days at a time, break the ice to admit air for the fish and other aquatic life.) Protect tropical water lilies by lowering them in the pool, so they will be covered by fifteen to twenty inches of water, or pack them in tubs and store in the basement. If stored, be sure they are kept well moist at all times.

Many Southern gardeners make a mistake by pruning their deciduous flowering shrubs in early winter. Early pruning encourages new growth, which will almost always be killed by later freezes. February is early enough to do your winter pruning in the Middle South. Pruning of the early spring-flowering shrubs now will remove the flower buds, of course, and the crop of flowers will be cut short.

December is a good time to apply a dormant spray, but select a time when the temperature is well above freezing. Spray all things susceptible to scale, including both fruiting and flowering peaches, lilacs, Japanese quinces, flowering almonds, the various cherries, spireas and roses. You will find it much better to get the prepared spray at your garden store than to attempt to mix your own.

You may patch up bad spots in the lawn this month, restoring the sod and planting rye grass for quick effects, but it is not the best time to plant new lawns in the South. In Florida and along the Gulf Coast, wait until March; in other areas, early April will be early enough to start.

Give the winter grass its first cutting when it is about three inches high, and don't cut too close. While the grass should be well established before the first mowing, it is a mistake to wait until it is several inches high; early mowing makes for good coverage.

Build feeding stations for the birds and put out food for them. If you cannot find time to build the feeders or stations, just use an old baking tin—anything to hold the food—but be sure it is out of reach of cats. The wild-bird grain feed found at the larger food stores is relished by practically all birds, and they dearly love peanut butter smeared into a large pine cone and hung to a tree branch with wire.

If snow weighs down branches of the evergreens, wash it off with the hose. The wind may split snow-bent branches, many times causing serious injury to the trees. You may use a rake or pitchfork to remove some of the snow, but you had better be very careful; otherwise you may break the frozen branches. Water from the hose will melt snow and ice without damage.

Cutting mistletoe for Christmas decorations does no harm to the trees from which it is removed. Mistletoe is a parasitic plant, and its removal is probably beneficial to the tree from which it is cut.

INDOOR GARDENING

Sudden changes from the greenhouse, where humidity and temperature can be controlled, to the variety of home conditions is responsible for many holiday gift **house plants** becoming ill and losing their foliage. Sudden changes in temperature can cause leaves of poinsettias, in particular, to yellow and fall. Foliage plants like ficus, Chinese evergreen, pothos and philodendron require much water. If your home is too warm, daily sprinklings of the plants will help. (See Chapter 27.)

Although Christmas cacti will tolerate lots of shade, they bloom best when given some sunlight, especially just prior to and during the blooming season. At this season they should be able to take full sun. Given sun now and adequately fed and watered, they should be in full bloom for the holidays. Do not overwater. Use liquid fertilizer according to directions.

A **terrarium** is not difficult to build. Many times you can pick up excellent large-mouthed glass containers at the junk yard or at some of the larger grocery stores. Some of the garden stores are now stocking lovely glass containers with covers which are suitable.

Place about an inch and a half of medium-size gravel in the bottom to drain away any excess water which might accumulate in watering; then an inch of half-and-half mixture of sand and peat moss; on top of this, the same quantity of half-and-half soil and peat moss; and last, about an inch of sphagnum moss. Wet down lightly and then place the plants, working the roots down into the soil mixture.

Many gardens, especially the older ones, will furnish generous supplies of material: little rooted tips of ivy of several kinds, an assortment of ajuga, tiny bits of ferns, little pieces of ground-clinging euonymus, little cuttings, like pieces of variegated ligustrum and, if you can find them, some pieces of partridgeberry with their red fruits. To add color, tuck in tiny branches of pyracantha and holly, carrying their red fruits. Now sprinkle lightly with water, to help settle the plants into their growing medium, and cover. If growth appears too rapid, you may leave off the cover of the container for one or more days at a time. Little plant food will be needed, but when used it should be applied in liquid form.

PLANTING LIST FOR DECEMBER

Seeds

*Ageratum
Alyssum
Anchusa
Baby blue-eyes
  (Nemophila)
Calendula
California poppy
  (Eschscholtzia)
Calliopsis
Candytuft (Iberis)
Carnation
  (Dianthus)

Chinese
  forget-me-not
  (Cynoglossum)
Coreopsis, perennial
Cornflower
  (Centaurea)
Feverfew
Gaillardia
Larkspur
Lupine
Nierembergia
Pansy

Phlox, annual
Poppy, Shirley
Queen Anne's lace
Snapdragon
  (Antirrhinum)
Stock
Strawflower
  (Helichrysum)
Sweet pea
Sweet William
Verbena
Viola odorata

Bulbs, Rhizomes and Tubers

Agapanthus
Allium
Alstroemeria
Amaryllis
Anemone
Billbergia
Butterfly lily
  (Hedychium)
Calla lily
  (Zantedeschia)
Chionodoxa
Clivia (in pots)
Crinum
Daffodil (Narcissus)
Freesia
Fritillaria

Grape hyacinth
  (Muscari)
Hyacinth
Iris
  Bulbous
  Dutch
  Louisiana
  Siberian
  I. unguicularis
Ismene
Ixia
Liatris
Lilies, all except the
  Easter varieties
Liriope
Marica

Narcissus
Ornithogalum
Oxalis
Ranunculus
Red-hot poker
  (Kniphofia)
Scilla
Snowdrop
Snowflake
Spider lily
  (Hymenocallis)
Tulip
Wandflower
  (Sparaxis)
Watsonia

---

* Plant in protected beds.

Section 2

What to Plant in the Garden

13

Annuals

The term "annual," as most of us know, is applied to those flowers which complete their entire cycle of life—sprouting of seed, growing of stem, production of flowers and fruit—all in one year. In our garden plan, the annuals have a great many uses. Many times there are bare places in the perennial beds that may be tastefully filled in with annuals which will harmonize with any carefully designed plan. Even in the shrubbery beds and foundation plantings one often finds open spaces which may be filled with these quick-growing plants.

One of the greatest virtues of the annual flowers is their very rapid growth, enabling us to enjoy their beauty and fragrance under conditions not applicable to the other classes of plants.

Sometimes we acquire new quarters too late in the season for us to plant perennials and shrubs. Under such conditions, the quick-growing annuals may be relied upon to meet the situation in a very satisfactory manner. Many of them planted in the Middle South in July and August will give excellent bloom before the first frost.

A few packets of seed, carried along when we go to our summer cottages or camps, may be the means of transforming barren, unsightly premises into spots of coziness and color.

From the dainty little carpet of snow alyssum, an inch or two

in height, to the sunflower and cosmos, which grow to six or
more feet; from the feathery textured foliage of the California
poppy to the tropical leaves of the castor bean, we should be
able to find plants of the size and character of growth suitable
to almost every type of planting.

In color, the annuals run the gamut of all the shades, and the
most exacting gardener should be able to find varieties of color
for working out any desired scheme.

From the lists at the end of this chapter, you can easily find
groups of plants adapted to practically all conditions of garden
culture.

The seed is an embryo, rudimentary plant provided by nature
with a protective covering, and it usually contains sufficient food
elements to get the young plant off to a head start. With this
in mind we can easily see that seeds should be carefully handled.
The viability depends on how they are treated and also on the
varieties and species. If stored in a moist place with high humidity they will not retain their ability to germinate for very long,
but if kept in cool dry storage some may retain their viability
for several years. Stories are told that seeds of the lotus and
other plants found in Egyptian tombs were proved viable after
several centuries. Of course, I cannot vouch personally for these
stories.

The soil of seedbeds and flats should be as congenial as possible. The larger seeds may be planted in the beds where they
are to grow, but the very small ones are better planted in flats.
A convenient size for flats is about 12 inches wide, from 20 to
24 inches long and 3½ inches deep. Ideal flats can be usually
made of scrap lumber found around the house. Holes should be
provided in the bottom to ensure proper drainage. Shallow
flower pots, often called "azalea pans," make good little flats.

The soil for the seedbed or flat should be of such character
that it may be easily penetrated by the roots of the young seedlings; stiff soils tend to retard the tender roots. Usually, a good
seedbed medium can be made by mixing one part each of garden
loam, sifted peat moss and sand.

In removing little seedlings from the seedbed or flat to their
growing bed, lift them with a spoon or a small trowel, carrying

all the medium that will cling to the roots, and promptly transplant them.

The terms "tender" and "hardy" as applied to annuals are exceedingly variable. A plant may be tender in the Midwest and entirely hardy in Florida and along the Gulf Coast. Seeds of the tender annuals should not be placed in the soil until it is warm. Annuals classed as hardy are usually sufficiently cold-resistant to justify planting them in the fall. By planting at this time those that are suitable for such treatment, you will induce greater root growth, enabling the plants to grow more successfully through the hot, dry periods of late spring; these plants will come into bloom earlier and will bloom over longer periods than if planted in the spring.

For a main planting of annuals, it would be well to rely on well-known plants, those that are known to succeed in your particular locality. But at the same time almost all enthusiastic gardeners will certainly want to try out some new varieties each year.

A friend of mine has a small section of her garden which she has designated as her "experiment station." It is only a bed located well back to the side where, each spring, she plants several species and varieties of seed which she has not previously grown. The bed is laid out in sections, and seeds are planted without regard to height or color; they are grown solely for experiment.

While the "All-America Selections" group has been in existence for several years, not all gardeners seem to be familiar with the functions of this organization. W. Ray Hastings, Executive Secretary of the group, advises:

> All-America Selections are the results of the only authentic preintroductory testing and comparative rating of new flower and vegetable seed varieties for North America. Sponsored by the garden seed industry of the United States and Canada, entries are from private, commercial and public institution plant breeders from around the free world. AAS is a non-profit educational institution, self-perpetuated by its Council of Judges who are responsible for their trial grounds and evaluations of merit and behavior of each entry under their climatic and soil conditions.

Awards are made annually to outstanding varieties of both flowers and vegetables. These award-winning varieties are very much in demand.

Seeds may usually be obtained from your seed catalog or from the local seed store. As a rule, most AAS annuals are easy to grow. Give them good soil, a fair amount of sunshine and moisture, and they will usually respond with a good crop of flowers.

ANNUALS USUALLY REGARDED AS TENDER

Ageratum
Amaranthus
Arctotis
Aster
Balsam
 (Impatiens)
Blue laceflower
 (Trachymene or
 Didiscus)
Browallia
Castor bean
 (Ricinus)
Cockscomb
 (Celosia)
Cosmos

Cuphea
Dimorphotheca
Gilia
Globe amaranth
 (Gomphrena)
Godetia
Kochia
Lobelia
Marigold
Mignonette
Moonflower
 (Calonyction)
Morning glory
Nasturtium
Nemesia
Nicotiana

Portulaca
Queen Anne's lace
Salpiglossis
Salvia
Sanvitalia
Schizanthus
Strawflower
 (Helichrysum)
Sunflower
 (Helianthus)
Tithonia
Torenia
Tulip poppy
 (Hunnemannia)
Zinnia

ANNUALS USUALLY REGARDED AS HARDY

Alyssum
Baby's-breath
 (Gypsophila)
Calendula
California poppy
 (Eschscholtzia)
Calliopsis
Candytuft (Iberis)
Chrysanthemum,
 annual
Clarkia

Cleome
Cornflower
 (Centaurea)
Crotalaria
Chinese
 forget-me-not
 (Cynoglossum)
English daisy
Flax (Linum)
Gaillardia
Hollyhock
Larkspur

Linaria
Lupine
Nigella
Pansy
Petunia
Phlox, annual
Poppy
Scabiosa
Statice
Stock
Sweet pea

ANNUALS SUITABLE FOR EDGING

Alyssum
Little Gem
Carpet of Snow
Calendula

California poppy
(Eschscholtzia)
Candytuft (Iberis)
Dimorphotheca
English daisy
Marigold, dwarf

Nasturtium, dwarf
Pansy
Petunia
Phlox drummondii
Portulaca

ANNUALS FOR HOT, DRY SITUATIONS

Amaranthus
California poppy
(Eschscholtzia)
Cornflower
(Centaurea)

Dimorphotheca
Gaillardia
Iceplant
(Cryophytum)
Nasturtium

Periwinkle
(*Vinca rosea*)
Phlox drummondii
Portulaca
Sanvitalia

ANNUALS FOR MOIST SITUATIONS

Ionopsidium   Mimulus

ANNUALS FOR SHADY SITUATIONS

Alyssum
Aster
Balsam
(Impatiens)
Chinese
forget-me-not
(Cynoglossum)

Clarkia
English daisy
Forget-me-not
(Myosotis)
Godetia
Lupine
Mimulus
Nicotiana

Pansy
Schizanthus
Snapdragon
(Antirrhinum)
Sweet sultan
(*Centaurea
moschata*)

ANNUALS FOR THE CUTTING GARDEN

Amaranthus
Aster
Baby's-breath
(Gypsophila)
Calliopsis
Carnation
(Dianthus)

Chrysanthemum,
annual
Cornflower
(Centaurea)
Everlasting
Gaillardia
Globe amaranth
(Gomphrena)

Godetia
Larkspur
Lupine
Marigold
Mignonette
Nasturtium
Pansy
Phlox

ANNUALS FOR THE CUTTING GARDEN (cont.)

Salpiglossis
Snapdragon
 (Antirrhinum)
Statice

Stock
Sunflower
 (Helianthus)
Sweet pea

Sweet sultan
 (*Centaurea
 moschata*)
Zinnia

ANNUALS OF MEDIUM GROWTH

Amaranthus
Calliopsis
Chinese
 forget-me-not
 (Cynoglossum)
Chrysanthemum,
 annual

Cornflower
 (Centaurea)
Godetia
Kochia
Larkspur
Marigold, African
Poppy

Snow-on-the-
 mountain
 (*Euphorbia
 marginata*)
Strawflower
 (Helichrysum)
Zinnia

TALL-GROWING ANNUALS SUITABLE FOR BACKGROUNDS AND SCREENS

Castor bean
 (Ricinus)

Cosmos
Marigold

Sunflower
 (Helianthus)
Tithonia

ANNUALS SUITABLE FOR ROCKERIES

Ageratum
Alyssum
Baby's-breath
 (Gypsophila)
Candytuft (Iberis)
Carnation
 (Dianthus)

Gaillardia
Ionopsidium
Linaria
Mimosa
Phlox drummondii
Portulaca
Schizanthus

Sedum
Sweet William
Thunbergia
Tulip poppy
 (Hunnemannia)
Verbena

14

Biennials

Southern gardeners can greatly enhance the charm of their gardens by using more biennials. Many of them are high-quality flowers, ideally suited for low beds and borders and for the front of the perennial beds. Most of them are quite easy to handle, and none requires more than ordinary garden care.

While the term "biennial," as applied to plants, has a varied meaning, a biennial, strictly according to the book, is one that requires two years for its cycle of growth (the production of stem, flower and seed).

Plants generally recognized as biennial in the South include Canterbury bells, English daisies, evening primroses (oenothera), forget-me-nots, foxgloves, hollyhocks, Iceland poppies, linarias, mulleins, pansies, Sweet Williams and wallflowers, but the list varies with the climate. A plant that falls in one group in the North may be placed in a different one in the South. Some plants considered perennial in colder areas become biennial in the South; some biennials of the North and Midwest are handled as hardy annuals in the warmer areas.

If the seeds of pansies are planted in the fall, for example, they will bloom the following winter and spring; plants from fall-planted seed may be set out as late as January or February for good spring bloom. The same is true of English daisies.

Since most plants included in the true biennial group are short-lived, it is the custom to grow them from seed each year, usually planted in summer or early fall. The seedlings may be transferred to their growing stations when they have reached a size that permits easy handling, or they may be left in the seed-beds or cold frames until winter if they do not crowd. Of course, the winter-flowering biennials like English daisies and pansies should be transferred to their permanent places as soon as the seedlings are large enough to be handled.

It is possible to carry over plants of some biennials and have them bloom a second season, but the plants usually lose much of their vigor and the bloom is rarely as good as it is the first season of bloom. It is better garden practice to remove the old plants from the beds, after they have flowered, and plant seeds every year to supply fresh vigorous plants. A few species can be propagated from offsets, cuttings or slips, but you will usually get better results if you plant seeds for an entirely new crop. Several of the biennials self-sow and perpetuate themselves with little effort on the gardener's part.

We can enjoy many of the perennials if we treat them as biennials, although they will not attain the stately size they do in a more congenial environment. Delphiniums, the perennial larkspur, which grow to the size of hollyhocks in the Canadian Rockies, may not reach over two or three feet in the South, but they add a note of novelty to the garden and give us some rich colors seldom found in other plants.

In treating perennials as biennials, plant seeds in the summer or fall, or buy the youngest plants you can find; divisions of old plants rarely give good results. The most common error in growing biennials is in planting them in the spring as we do annuals. Spring is definitely not the time to plant. Late summer and fall is the proper time; this gives time for the plants to form little rosettes of leaves before winter arrives. If you buy young plants, do not wait too late to order them. The spring-flowering ones (this includes nearly all biennials) can be set out almost any time from early winter to early spring, but as a rule the earlier they are planted in the garden the better they will do. Planted

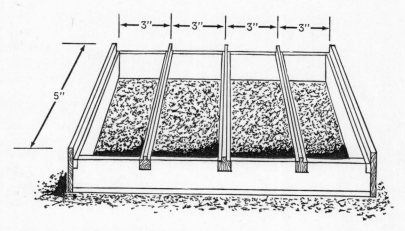

A neat seedbed can usually be made from scraps of lumber found about the house.

early, they will start putting out growth and making new roots immediately, to prepare for their display of flowers as soon as spring makes its appearance.

The seedbed for biennials should be well prepared. A mixture of equal parts of garden soil, sand and screened peat moss makes a very congenial soil. Wet down the bed, then sow the seeds and cover them lightly with sand or some of the soil mixture suggested for the bed. Make the bed in light shade and cover it with burlap or paper until the seeds begin to sprout; then remove the covering. Sprinkle the young plants lightly and often enough to keep the soil moist. Be sure to transplant the seedlings before they begin to crowd. Give them room to develop into strong, stocky plants; feed and water them. Only good plants will give good flowers.

15

Perennials

Technically, a plant that lives for more than two years qualifies as a perennial. But to most gardeners, especially in the South, the term is applied to those plants which wholly or partially die out in the winter and come up again from the same root system in the spring.

We can grow many good perennial flowers in the Middle South. While a few of the more dependable ones, like the old blue and white "flags" or iris, pinks, and some others have been with us since the early days of gardening in the South, each generation has been told that, generally, we could not grow perennials down here.

It is quite true that many fine perennials that have long formed the backbone of home gardens in the colder areas will not thrive in the Middle South. It seems that they require a longer rest period and harder winter cold than is permitted by our mild, short winters. They become very unhappy and usually fade out in two or three years; some do not last that long.

But in recent years quite a bit of experimenting has been done, and by the old system of trial and error we have found that many perennials which we had been told for years would not succeed here actually do very well, especially if a little extra

114

attention is given them. It seems natural that when a person locates in a different section of the country he will want to try to grow the things he grew back home. Many people who have moved from the Midwest and New England into the warm Southland have lost little time in proving to us that many of their favorite Northern flowers can be grown down here.

It is suggested, however, that those families who have recently moved from colder areas into warmer ones first learn from local gardeners what species and varieties are known to thrive in their new location and use this information as a basis for their major plantings. Most all of us like to experiment, and we gain much from it, but whether it be in business, horticulture or human relationships it should be conducted with due caution.

Some of these perennials may require special selection as to species and varieties, and in some cases a bit of special cultural treatment. But with this added attention we can succeed with a surprisingly large number of them.

Gardeners in the South, especially in the Deep South, have long depended on annuals for the major portion of their color. In many cases the herbaceous perennials are almost, if not entirely, lacking in the garden design. We should improve this situation, as well-selected perennials will add much to the bloom practically all through the year. One great advantage of perennial plantings is their permanency. Once planted in good soil and given proper culture, most of them may be left entirely alone for from two to four years.

Dr. John V. Watkins of the Florida Experiment Station states in a bulletin on perennials:

Herbaceous perennials are most valuable in bold, loosely planted mass for color effect, and are much more pleasing when grown this way, rather than when spotted about with a great deal of distance between the plants. Growing perennials subordinate to shrubbery in drifts or large clumps is considered one of the best arrangements. Since perennials stay in the beds for more than one year they should be well supplied with materials which release nutrients slowly, over a long period.

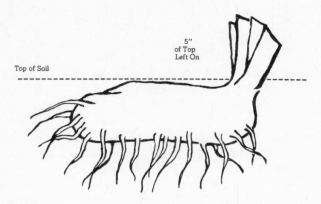

5"
of Top
Left On

Top of Soil

Bearded irises should be planted in full sunlight with the rhizomes barely covered.

In order to get at least a semblance of the effect of mass, it is usually best to plant at least three perennials of a kind in a clump, placing them in a triangular position. If the plants are of a small-growing species, five plants to the clump would probably be better.

Many perennials are easily grown from seed, but most of them do not "come true," and in order to get a certain variety it is necessary to use plants grown from cuttings or divisions.

When seeds are used they may be planted at almost any time during the growing season, but spring planting is preferred for most species. In the case of irises and daylilies, the seeds should be planted just as soon as they are ripe.

A question of how far south peonies can be successfully grown is one of long standing. Gilbert H. Wild & Son of Sarcoxie, Missouri, perhaps the largest grower of peonies, daylilies and bearded irises in the entire country, has issued a very informative bulletin on the culture of peonies in the South. This bulletin quoted a grower of long experience, living in north Alabama, in which he stated that if the climate is mild enough for successful growing of the Maréchal Niel rose, it is too warm for the successful growing of peonies. With this I agree.

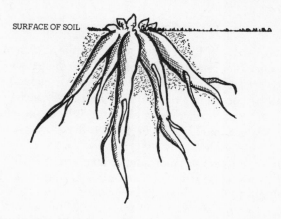

SURFACE OF SOIL

When planting peonies in the South, place the crown just level with the surface of the soil.

Of course, no definite geographical lines can be drawn. We cannot say that you can grow peonies north of a certain line and cannot grow them south of it. However, after observation and some research made over the last three decades, I am of the opinion that, generally speaking, peonies may be grown in most areas north of the old U.S. Highway 80 but in few communities south of that highway. This would mean, roughly speaking, that a line drawn from Dallas via Marshall, Vicksburg, Jackson, Meridian, Montgomery and to the east would roughly separate the growing from the nongrowing peony areas.

Here in Meridian we are on this line and have several gardens in town where peonies are grown with great success. Other local gardeners have not succeeded nearly as well.

The Wilds' bulletin gives some pertinent suggestions as to planting and other points in culture. The general planting instructions state that peonies should be planted with the crown two inches under the soil level, but this bulletin on growing peonies in the South states that down here we should plant our peonies with the eyes at the ground level. I think these instructions relative to the depth of planting are highly important. The peony is a cold-weather plant and freezing and light freezes will do the roots no harm; in fact, hard cold seems to be essential to the production of blooms.

The Wilds' bulletin further suggests that the reason why many peonies do not bloom is they are planted too deep. Also the buds are sometimes killed by frost or attacked by thrips or disease. Plants may be too young to bloom or be undernourished. Sometimes they are undermined by moles, and in some situations they may be given too much shade or get too dry during the summer and fall.

It is suggested that, in planting, a hole about eighteen inches deep and as wide be dug for each peony. The subsoil encountered in digging, if it is clay or very sandy, should be discarded and replaced with a good garden soil with which a small quantity of leaf mold or peat moss has been mixed. In a hole of the size suggested, there is great danger of the plant sinking too low unless the soil in the bottom of the hole is well packed before the plant is set.

I have been experimenting with peonies for many years and find the single-flowering, the Japanese varieties and the very earliest of the double-flowering varieties best for the South. The *officinalis* hybrid varieties are also recommended for planting here. Of course, as we travel north from the Highway 80 line, the climate for growing good peonies increases in desirability. I saw, a few years ago, in Corinth, Mississippi, a few miles south of the Tennessee line, some of the finest peonies I have ever seen anywhere.

The principal disease affecting peonies in the South is botrytis blight, which also affects many other plants in the garden. It is evidenced in the case of peonies by all parts of the plant being affected. New shoots may suddenly turn black and die. Bordeaux mixture or any other good fungicide should help control the disease. Spraying should begin as soon as the plants peep through the surface.

LOW-GROWING PERENNIALS SUITABLE FOR BORDERS

Ajuga	Astilbe	Festuca
Alyssum	Candytuft (Iberis)	Geum
Arabis	Carnation	Iceland poppy
Armeria	(Dianthus)	(*Papaver nudicaule*)

Iris, dwarf
Nierembergia
Painted daisy
  (Pyrethrum)
Phlox, dwarf

Plumbago
  (Ceratostigma)
Saxifrage
Scabiosa
Sedum in variety

Snow-in-summer
  (Cerastium)
Statice
Stokesia
Veronica, dwarf
Violet (Viola)

PERENNIALS OF MEDIUM HEIGHT

Achillea
Agapanthus
Alstroemeria
Artemisia
Baby's-breath
  (Gypsophila)
Baptisia
Chrysanthemum
Columbine
  (Aquilegia)
Coreopsis

Daisy
Daylily
  (Hemerocallis)
Dicentra
Digitalis
Eupatorium
Gaillardia
Iris
Liatris
Linaria
Lupine

Lychnis
Monarda
Pentstemon
Peony
Phlox
Physostegia
Poppy
Red-hot poker
  (Kniphofia)
Salvia
Sedum spectabile

TALL PERENNIALS SUITABLE FOR BACKGROUNDS

Boltonia
Coneflower
  (Rudbeckia)
Eulalia

Helenium
Hibiscus
Michaelmas daisy
  (Aster)

Lathyrus (vine)
Sunflower
  (Helianthus)
Yucca filamentosa

PERENNIALS FOR SOMEWHAT MOIST SITUATIONS

Boltonia asteroides
Cardinal flower
  (*Lobelia*
  cardinalis)
Eulalia japonica
Eupatorium
  purpureum
Ferns in variety
Forget-me-not
  (Myosotis)

Helenium
  autumnale
Iris
  Louisiana
  Yellow flag
  I. versicolor
Lily-of-the-valley
  (Convallaria)
Lythrum

Primrose (Primula)
Rose mallow
  (*Hibiscus*
  moscheutos)
Spider lily
  (Hymenocallis)
Typha latifolia

PERENNIALS FOR DRY, SUNNY SITUATIONS

Achillea
Anthemis
Asclepias
Baby's-breath
  (Gypsophila)
Callirhoë
Carnation
  (Dianthus)

Coneflower
  (Rudbeckia)
Coreopsis
Cornflower
  (Centaurea)
Daylily
  (Hemerocallis)
Doronicum
Echinops

Gaillardia
Heliopsis
Iris, bearded
Lychnis
Opuntia
Poppy
Sunflower
  (Helianthus)
Yucca

PERENNIALS FOR SHADY SITUATIONS

Ajuga
Anemone
Aster
Balloon flower
  (*Platycodon
grandiflorum*)
Blue phlox
  (*P. divaricata*)
Columbine
  (Aquilegia)
Coneflower
  (Rudbeckia)
Daylily
  (Hemerocallis)

Eupatorium
Ferns in variety
Goldenrod
Hosta
Hypericum
Lily-of-the-valley
  (Convallaria)
Lobelia
Lychnis
Lythrum
Monarda
Physostegia
Primrose (Primula)

Red-hot poker
  (Kniphofia)
Rose mallow
  (*Hibiscus
moscheutos*)
Sedum in variety
Thalictrum
Trillium
Veronica
Violet (Viola)
Virginia bluebells
  (*Mertensia
virginica*)

PERENNIALS FOR CONTINUOUS BLOOM

Spring

Anchusa
Cerastium
Columbine
  (Aquilegia)
Coreopsis
Daylily
  (Hemerocallis)

Carnation
  (Dianthus)
Hepatica
Iceland poppy
  (*Papaver
nudicaule*)
Iris
Peony

Phlox
  P. divaricata
  P. subulata
Primrose (Primula)
Veronica
Virginia bluebells
  (*Mertensia
virginica*)

Summer

Anthemis
Asclepias
Baby's-breath
  (Gypsophila)
Balloon flower
  (*Platycodon
  grandiflorum*)
Baptisia
Bellflower
  (Campanula)
Blue salvia
Boltonia

Daylily
  (Hemerocallis)
Eupatorium
Gaillardia
Gas plant
  (*Dictamnus
  albus*)
Japanese anemone
Liatris
Mallow (Malva)
Malvaviscus
Monkshood
  (Aconitum)

Oriental poppy
  (*Papaver
  orientale*)
Pentstemon
Phlox
Physostegia
Sedum spectabile
Shasta daisy
Stokesia
Sunflower
  (Helianthus)
Veronica

Fall

Asters in variety
Chrysanthemums
  in variety
Coreopsis

Daylily
  (Hemerocallis)
Eupatorium
Gaillardia

Goldenrod
Lobelia
Monarda
Phlox

16

Chrysanthemums

The chrysanthemum is one of our oldest flowers. History tells us that it was mentioned by Confucius in his writings some 500 years B.C. During all these centuries it has suffered many declines in popularity, but it always comes back with greater force and vitality than it had previously experienced.

PROPAGATION

My grandmother, some three score and ten years ago, had many garden "pinks," as they were then called, that she had planted forty years before, when her parents settled in that location. As I recall it, these "pinks" were never watered, sprayed or given other cultural attention except to have an application of well-rotted barnyard manure about once a year. This garden practice, however, was for the past, not the present. Present-day varieties subjected to such treatment would survive only a season or two.

To reduce the incidence of insects and disease, it is far better to grow entirely new plants from cuttings each season. If you divide the old clumps you will carry with the plants any disease present. Chrysanthemums, due to their herbaceous, woody root systems, are highly susceptible to attacks from termites when sections of the old plants are used in propagation, especially in the Deep South. Since they are so easily rooted from cuttings, the growth of new plants is no problem.

In the spring when the new growth is about two or three inches in height, clip it off and root in a medium of half sand and half peat moss. Instructions on rooting cuttings given in Chapter 25 apply to chrysanthemums as well.

Chrysanthemum cuttings are so easily rooted that, if they are placed in full shade, many will root in two or three weeks without being covered; however, rooting will be hastened if the tray or flat is covered with a sheet of plastic.

GARDEN TYPES

The garden chrysanthemum is of extraordinarily easy culture and offers an unusual opportunity for gardeners throughout the South to make their landscapes bright and colorful during the autumn months. Its popularity extends from Florida and south Texas northward throughout the country.

The mountainous areas of the Upper South offer many opportunities for making hillside plantings of garden chrysanthemums that in brilliance and boldness of color could vie with the azalea plantings of the Gulf Coast.

Practically all of the garden types are well adapted for use throughout the South, but the widely exploited azaleamums seem to be more at home in the Upper South than in the Middle and Deep South. In the Meridian area most of them tend to begin flowering too early, sometimes in August or September. The bloom is many times produced sparingly over a long period, and we do not get the great mass of color that this form presents farther north, but we are not lacking in many lovely varieties of the conventional garden types to give us adequate autumn color.

Pinching. In all my many years of gardening and garden travels, I have seen few plantings of garden-type chrysanthemums that I considered adequately pinched. Pinching should start by removing the terminal buds when the plants are three or four inches high and should continue after each three or four inches of growth is made. This means that several pinchings would be made during the season of growth of the plant. Discontinue pinching early varieties in early autumn; late varieties, a few weeks later.

Several successive pinchings will result in much heavier growth and bloom. It will produce plants with more sturdy and stocky development, which will need little or no staking. If, however, you failed to pinch the plants adequately, be sure to stake and tie them up before they fall down and develop crooked stems.

Feeding and Watering. Chrysanthemums demand quite a bit of food and moisture, and it is well for all types to be fed every two to four weeks and watered with sufficient frequency to maintain adequate moisture. I prefer one of the several liquid plant foods now available at the garden stores. Continue feeding until color begins to show in the blooms.

Suggested Varieties. The chrysanthemum planting at Callaway Gardens located at Pine Mountain, Georgia, developed under the supervision of Dr. Fred Galle, Director of Horticulture, is one of the few outstanding plantings of this flower in the South. The Callaway people recommend the following garden varieties:

Bronze

Carnival	Lawrence Blaney	Red Skin
Cheyenne	Pumpkin	Indian Summer
Dark Calumet	Scarleteer	Roll Call
Huntsman	(fade-resistant)	

Pink

Ann Ladygo	Raspberry Ice	Minnpink
Margo	Tinker Bell	September Song
Cameo	Mischief	Spellbound
No. 2 Fuchsia Fairy		

Yellow

Yellow Chris	Tranquility (or	Top Flight
Columbus	Golden	Chiquita
Astoria	Tranquility)	King's Ransom
Yellow Calumet	Gay Blade	Golden Peking

White

Sleigh Ride	Corsage Cushion	Powder River
Chris Columbus	Larry	

DECORATIVE TYPES

There is a kind of chrysanthemum called "decorative" which comes in between the hardy garden types and the mammoth exhibition types. They are largely used by florists to provide us with potted chrysanthemums almost the entire year. They are ideal for growing in small pots, and the home gardener should have no trouble in growing specimens that will rival those seen in the florists' shops.

The procedure is to take well-rooted cuttings and pot them up about the first of July, using from three to five cuttings to the pot. Then, when the plants are about four inches high, the buds should be pinched off. This will result in each plant putting on several branches. It is customary to leave about four of these branches to each plant. Each branch should give a nice bloom; thus a pot containing five plants, four branches to each plant, would give twenty nice flowers and fill a five- or six-inch pot.

EXHIBITION TYPES

Did you ever stop in front of a florist's window around Thanksgiving to marvel at the mammoth "mums" and wish you could grow them yourself? Well, you can. With just a little effort you can grow, right in your own garden, giant chrysanthemums that will rival in both size and beauty those produced in greenhouses.

The culture of exhibition-type chrysanthemums differs somewhat from that of the hardy garden types, but it is not too complicated. The cuttings can be planted any time during the spring —March to early June—but mid-spring is the best time for planting most varieties in the Middle South.

Since these flowers are gross feeders, the soil for them should be rich and deep. Spade the ground to a depth of eight or ten inches, but before working it, apply a rather heavy layer of leaf mold, peat moss and dehydrated cow manure, or a lighter one of sheep manure. If you can't get the manure, use about three pounds of good commercial garden fertilizer (6–8–8) to each hundred feet of row or hundred square feet of bed. Regardless of the type of plant food used, work it well into the soil with a fork or potato rake.

The plants may be grown in rows in the vegetable area or in beds. Space them twelve to twenty inches apart, depending somewhat on the variety and the number of canes left to each plant. The less vigorous varieties like Chrysalora can be spaced twelve inches apart when only one or two canes are left to the plant; vigorous ones like the Turner's and Indianapolis varieties should have a full twenty inches when grown, with three or four canes to the plant.

Pinching. If you plant exhibition varieties in mid-spring, pinch out the buds when the plants have made three or four pairs of new leaves. After being pinched they will begin to produce new branches or canes. It is at this time that you must decide just how many flowers you want from each plant. Leave one cane for each flower and pinch off all the others. If only one cane is left to each plant, the flower should be larger, but most of the large-flowered kinds, if not planted too late, are capable of producing three or four huge flowers, and you may leave that number of canes per plant. But if the plants are set out very late, or if they are very weak, do not attempt to grow more than one or two blooms to the plant.

Many of the plants set out in the spring will show immature terminal flower buds in June. If they do, pinch out the buds, as

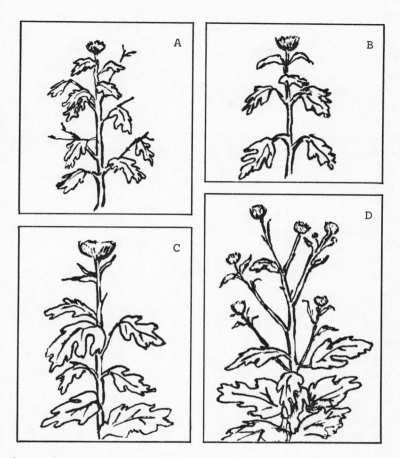

Chrysanthemum showing: A, crown bud with side branches; B, the same plant with side branches removed; C, the plant three weeks later; and D, clusters of terminal buds.

they will never open into good flowers. New shoots should appear right under the spot where the immature flower bud grew; leave one of these new side shoots to form a new terminal to produce flowers. After five or six weeks another bud will appear. This is called a crown bud because it forms in the very top of the cane and is surrounded by a circle of bracts. If the crown buds appear much before September 1 on midseason varieties, they also must be pinched off, for coming that early they will not develop into good flowers. If and when they are removed, a side shoot just below should be left to grow and produce another bud.

If the crown buds are removed, there will later appear in the terminal of each cane a cluster of flower buds called terminal buds. These will be the last buds produced for the season, and one of them must be left for the flower. The others should be pinched off when they are about the size of peas or a little larger. Normally, the bud in the center of the cluster is the best one and the one that should be saved.

Cuttings that are put out very late may not produce crown buds but, instead, will produce terminal buds in autumn, one of which should be selected for the flower.

The most important phase of growing mammoth chrysanthemums is keeping the canes pruned and disbudded. Regardless of everything else, you will get only mediocre flowers unless you keep the side shoots pinched off. In late summer and fall they will appear almost like magic, and the plants will require pruning at least once each week. Pinch off these developing side branches just as soon as they are long enough to be reached with the fingers.

Feeding and Watering. Even though your soil is good and was well enriched before planting, give the plants several feedings during the season. Liquid fertilizer used as directed on the label is usually quite effective. Watering, too, is very important. Do not overwater, but see that the earth is kept moist at all times.

Large-flowered chrysanthemums respond favorably to mulches. Any of the several mulch materials will be all right, and very good results have been achieved by using mulch paper, or ordinary black building paper, spread between the rows. Pine straw is also very good.

Do not be misled by the blooming dates shown in the catalogs of northern growers, for dates of bloom vary greatly with the latitude. A given variety will probably bloom a week later in Shreveport and Meridian than in Asheville and Louisville, but several days later in New Orleans and Houston than in Shreveport and Meridian. Blooming dates are actually influenced by the length of the days and nights; long nights induce bloom. If night is simulated by covering the plants with dark cloth, blooming will be hastened.

Insects and Diseases. The chief insect enemy of chrysanthemums in most sections of the South is the cucumber beetle, which attacks the plants when in bloom and feeds on the blooms themselves. Spraying with any dependable contact insecticide at weekly intervals, from the time the first color begins to show in the blooms until they are well open, usually gives good control.

The next most important insect is the termite, already mentioned. When termites attack there may be no evidence of their presence until early autumn, when the whole plant, many times in full flower bud, suddenly wilts and dies. When this stage is reached, there is nothing that can be done except to take up the plant with the roots and burn it, as the termites are in the roots and cannot be reached by insecticides.

There are not many diseases that attack chrysanthemums in this area, but one important disease is blight that begins by scorching and burning of the leaves near the ground and rapidly moves upward until practically all the plant loses its foliage. If treatment is begun in time, a reliable fungicide will prove effective.

17

Dahlias

When explorers and settlers first arrived in America, they found numerous plants they had not known in the Old World. Some of these new plants were colorful, lovely and enchanting and made strong appeal to the Europeans. During the first centuries many were introduced into European gardens, and some became immensely popular in a short time. The dahlia, however, discovered by the Spaniards on the volcanic plateaus of Mexico, although it was one of the first sent back home, was slow in gaining favor. The Spaniards discovered this genus about 1519, but there is no record of its growth in Europe until late in the eighteenth century.

The flowers found growing in the wild were mostly single in form, and it was some time before the dahlia as we know it today made its way into the better gardens of Europe. The first flowers discovered in their native habitat in Mexico, over four hundred years ago, bore little resemblance to the huge blooms now seen in our modern dahlia shows. In fact, history tells us that most of the forms of the modern dahlia now so popular have been developed since 1800, many of them during the last part of the past century.

Although the dahlia is native to the highlands of Mexico and seems to have thrived in that area, it will grow in almost any

130

soil where the drainage is perfect. If the soil in your garden is not conducive to growing good dahlias, it will not be difficult to make it so. Although the root is not a true tuber, the dahlia prefers a loose, friable soil.

Dahlias are propagated from seeds, cuttings and tubers. Seeds are generally used for the single and small-flowering varieties, but the seeds of the double do not always come true, and for this type tubers are generally used. Many times, in propagating a rare variety, cuttings are used. If treated as summer cuttings, they are quite easily rooted and may be started in a frame, lifted out and planted in a bed for later transfer to the garden.

Many cuttings may be produced from one plant by using the main stem as a cutting when it gets about six inches high, and then by taking additional cuttings from the side shoots when they are four or five inches long. One may continue taking cuttings, if needed, from the same plant until early summer. While planting the tuber is safe for the beginning gardener, it grows only one plant, as a rule.

For the tall-growing varieties each tuber will require a hole some twenty inches deep and twenty inches across. Fill in the bottom with about eight inches of prepared soil, which may be composed of three parts garden loam, two parts peat moss, and one part dehydrated sheep or cow manure. If the manure is not easily available you may use an ounce or two of commercial fertilizer. Be sure that the various ingredients are thoroughly mixed. Above this prepared soil, add an inch or two of unfertilized soil; place the tuber on top in horizontal position; then fill in with topsoil. Many dahlia growers make a practice of leaving a slight depression which may be filled in during the process of cultivation.

The tall-growing varieties will require staking, and the stake should usually be placed before the planting is done. Stakes of bamboo or steel may be purchased from the garden stores, or strips of lumber are sometimes found at the lumberyards which may be cut to the proper lengths and driven down a few inches from where the tuber will be placed. In my area it is necessary to treat all wood placed in the soil to prevent attack by termites.

If the stakes are painted green they will harmonize with the foliage and be less conspicuous.

As a rule, when tubers are used, only one sprout will be produced. If more than one should appear it may be pulled off, easily rooted in sand and treated like other summer cuttings.

For the largest blooms, plants must be disbudded and disbranched. One method is to let the first main stalk grow; this gives an early flower (which we are all anxious to get) with a good long stem. After this first flower is removed, other canes produced from the base of the leaves may be left on the stub, to be disbranched and disbudded later.

Another method is to pinch back the plant when it is about five or six inches long and then disbud and disbranch the resulting new growth.

In growing flowers for shows, only a few can be produced from each plant, and the disbranching should be very severely done. The flower buds are usually formed in clusters of threes. The gardener should pinch out two of these as soon as they are large enough to handle, leaving only the strongest one, which is usually the middle bud.

The plants should be tied to their stakes when they have attained a height of twenty-four to thirty inches. The tying up of the canes is essential if good straight stems are to be produced. In the case of plants that have been pinched back to form a low bushy development, less tying up will be needed.

Dahlias are gross feeders and will require considerable quantities of both moisture and food. From the time the first flower buds appear, the soil should be kept moist at all times. Several applications of plant food should be made during the season. One with a heavy content of potash and phosphate, analyzing about 6–10–10 or 6–12–12, usually gives good results.

In the Gulf Coast area, Zones 9 and 10, it is usually safe to leave tubers in the ground, but in Zone 8, the Middle South, they should always be given a heavy winter mulch of straw. In order to prevent breaking off the young sprouts, the clumps of tubers should be taken up and separated before they begin to sprout. By loosening the earth around the clump with a spade,

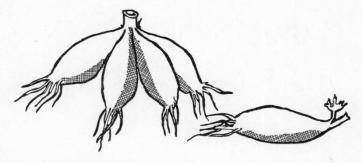

A clump of dahlia tubers attached to the old stem. In separating, nandle so that a section of the old stem is left with each tuber. It is on the "neck" of the old stem that the new plant will grow.

you may lift them out with a garden fork without injury to the tubers. The tubers, of course, are all attached to the old stem, and all the "eyes" are at the base of the old stalk. Try to split the old stalk in such a manner that a section of it will remain with each tuber. As indicated, the "eye," or bud, is on the neck of the tuber where it joins the old stem; if this eye is broken off through careless handling, the tuber will not grow another and is therefore worthless.

We used to recommend storing the tubers in a frost-proof cellar, but so many modern Southern homes do not have cellars that we will have to make another recommendation. If a heated garage or basement is available, it is recommended that the clumps be dug in the fall just after frost has killed the tops, packed in sand or peat moss and placed in the garage or basement. Sometimes the tubers have a tendency to dry out during winter storage; it is recommended that they be examined once or twice during midwinter and, if they appear to be shriveling too much, sprinkled with water so that the packing will be slightly moistened. They should not be kept wet, but damp.

As previously stated, these flowers are heavy users of moisture, and a heavy-foliaged plant loses a tremendous amount of it through transpiration. A good mulch will greatly reduce the amount of artificial watering required

18

Daylilies

Daylilies, or hemerocallis, have special appeal for gardeners who have little time to spend with their plants. With the heavy demands made on our time, many of us find far fewer hours to devote to our gardens than we would like; there is hardly time to do all the weeding, watering, feeding, spraying and cultivating necessary to keep things looking neat and trim.

Not many of us can afford any great amount of garden labor at prevailing prices, and what we do get is often sorely incompetent and inefficient. Some of us like to take vacations in the summer, and it is disheartening to return home after ten days or two weeks and find our plants, over which we labored so consistently for months, dead or dying for lack of water or other cultural attention.

Summing up all these things, we are forced to the conclusion that for the backbone or mainstay of our gardens we must tend to eliminate the frail, fastidious things that require constant attention and a bit of coddling and, instead, use material that is sufficiently rugged to take care of itself for weeks or months at a time, if need be, and that may be left unattended for long periods without serious injury.

Among the few dependable stalwarts you will find the daylily ranking near the top. They are as beautiful as any flower of the garden, and in the planting plan they have many and varied uses. All of the currently popular daylilies are hybrids whose parents, many generations removed, were species collected from the wild in the Orient. They came from widely varying geographical areas and altitudes. The species were first crossed to develop the first hybrids and then the hybrids were crossed and recrossed, again and again, in an effort to develop certain colors and flower forms. As a result the plants we have today are quite adaptable to varying situations with reference to soil, sun, shade and winter cold.

The present amazing interest in daylilies began right after the close of World War II and has gained in momentum each succeeding year. In 1934 there were approximately 175 named varieties, and in 1948 there were less than 300; but about that time gardeners everywhere began to wake up to the great possibilities of this flower. Professional horticulturists, hybridizers and run-of-the-field gardeners all became interested in trying their hands at producing new forms and colors.

When my book *Daylilies and How to Grow Them* was published in 1954, the number of registered varieties had jumped to nearly 4,000; the checklist issued by the American Hemerocallis Society in 1970 listed nearly 15,000 named varieties. I doubt if any flower in the history of ornamental horticulture has ever met with such astounding popular acceptance.

The exceptional interest in daylilies is not a fad or a craze. It is a recognition, long due, of a flower that has proved itself worthy of a permanent place in practically every American garden and definitely in every Middle South garden. In the Middle South, taken as a whole, the daylily is our most dependable perennial flower.

There is hardly an area where it does not give good growth and bloom, even under adverse cultural conditions, but good treatment of daylilies is definitely recommended. Since you normally do not expect to disturb them for several years, a big hole should be dug at planting time and the soil well enriched. They will certainly pay for this little extra attention, but if you find it necessary to neglect them you will encounter no great amount of resentment on their part. They will grow in any soil where other garden flowers thrive, in full sun or partial shade, even in deep shade if the light is good.

While commercial-sized daylilies should give at least one flower scape the first year, the clumps are not at their best until about the third or fourth season after planting. It is not until the clump is well developed and sends up eight to twelve flower stems, each with a dozen or more flower buds, that you can really appreciate the full beauty of any particular variety. Do not, therefore, be in too much of a hurry to divide your clumps. Some may object to the daylily because the blooms of most varieties close at the end of the day, but if you have a large clump that gives many new flowers every morning you will hardly realize that the individual bloom lasts for one day only.

The current trend of daylilies is toward clearer melons, pinks, reds and lavenders; some hybridists are trying for blues and pure whites. Even though the names of some varieties indicate such, there are as yet no white daylilies; neither have I seen one that I would call blue. While there are now a considerable number that remain open evenings, the hybridists are working hard to add to the list, as well as to add to the list of varieties that repeat bloom or bloom over an extended season.

The price of newly introduced daylilies has been the subject of some criticism. The asking price for many of them is very high, yet something can be said for the hybridizer. When, after working five years or longer, making thousands of crosses, keeping volumes of records, producing and disposing of countless inferior seedlings, he finally does come up with something outstanding, then waits three or four years to grow enough plants to be able to introduce it (after eight to ten years' work), do you not think he is justified in placing his price high enough to make a decent profit?

While I can now readily see where I wasted many years by using inferior parent plants, it was not until after more than ten years' work that I produced a seedling considered worthy of being named and registered.

If one is seriously interested in daylilies, he should join the American Hemerocallis Society. The secretary of this organization at the time of writing was Mrs. Lewis B. Wheeler, Jr., Box 586, Woodstock, Illinois 60098.

19

Azaleas and
Rhododendrons

Some years ago botanists officially discontinued the use of the name "azalea" and replaced it with "rhododendron." They now consider that all the plants commonly called azaleas are rhododendrons, that the genus Rhododendron includes all azaleas, and that the Latinized name of the Azalea series should be preceded by R. for *Rhododendron,* and not by A. for *Azalea,* as R. *indicum,* not A. *indicum.*

This confusion, I think, is unfortunate. Nurserymen here in the South, as well as everyday gardeners, still call azaleas by that name, reserving the term "Rhododendron" for the leathery or heavy-foliaged plants that produce bell-shaped or funnel-shaped flowers, mostly umbel-like racemes, making prominent autumnal buds. The dictionary states that the botanical difference between the two genera is not constant.

Some years ago an editorial committee composed of Frederic P. Lee, Fred O. Coe, B. Y. Morrison, Milo Perkins and Freeman Weiss was appointed by the American Horticultural Society to prepare an azalea handbook. This group was composed of the most eminent and knowledgeable azalea authorities in America. In the resulting publication, the editors, while acknowledging that rhododendrons had been substituted for azaleas by the botanists, proceeded to use the term "azalea" throughout the book.

To the everyday Southern gardener, an azalea may be either deciduous or evergreen, but they are always "azaleas" and never "rhododendrons." All of the species native to the South are deciduous, and all of the garden types in the South are evergreen.

Having conducted a small retail nursery business for several years, and having bought all of my stock from wholesalers on the Gulf Coast, I am fairly familiar with the terminology and nomenclature used in that area, for azaleas are produced there by the millions of plants each year. I have yet to hear a garden azalea called a rhododendron by either a nurseryman or gardener in the South. Inasmuch as both the nurseryman and the gardener continue to call the azalea series by that name, we also will continue to use it in our writings.

AZALEAS

In some sections of the South the soil will need conditioning, but there are few sections indeed where, with a little preparation, azaleas cannot be successfully grown.

In an old abandoned garden in the long-leaf pine belt, some thirty miles north of Mobile, there are specimen plants of azaleas now more than a century old. Some plants have layered naturally and produced new plants, layering again and again until the mass measures some 130 feet in circumference and is perhaps fifteen feet or more in height. This old planting has grown up in pine, gum and oak and for a half century has had no attention from man, yet these plants, without artificial watering or feeding —with no attention whatever, in fact—have gone on from decade to decade, not only holding their own but increasing in size and vigor.

The true glory of the azaleas is best revealed in the many old gardens of the South, where plants a hundred years old or older may be found.

SPECIES OF AZALEAS

If we needed other evidence of the adaptability of our Southern conditions to the culture of azaleas, it could be found in the species of the native plants which abound in numerous localities.

Indicas.   *Azalea indica* is perhaps the best known of the different types. The authorities tell us, however, that no azalea is indigenous to India and that the name is a misnomer. The shrub probably came from China or Japan.

The Indicas, as they are commonly called, are large-leaf, large-flowered, and under satisfactory conditions are fast growing. They are perhaps the tenderest of the azalea series except the Belgians, but may be grown outdoors, as a rule, where temperatures do not fall below 15 to 20 degrees. Low temperature may not materially injure large established plants but may damage the flower buds. In my own garden, well-established plants of Formosa and Pride of Mobile have stood temperatures of two degrees above zero and come through with little injury, although the crop of flower buds was severely damaged. A popular and dependable variety of the Indicas is Pride of Mobile, the azalea that made Mobile famous: a fast grower, with good foliage, watermelon pink in color. This azalea is more widely planted, perhaps, than any other in the South.

Kurumes.   This group, botanically *Azalea abrusum japonicum*, includes the small-leaf, compact-growing varieties which have proved perfectly hardy. It is our understanding that they are grown outdoors as far north as New York.

The Kurume azaleas first gained public attention in 1920 when the Massachusetts Horticultural Society held an exhibition, representing approximately 120 plants in fifty named varieties. According to a bulletin of that organization, these azaleas were found by Dr. E. H. Wilson at Kurume, on the Island of Kyushu, Japan, in 1918. Dr. Wilson arranged for fifty-two of the best sorts, in duplicates, to be shipped to the Arnold Arboretum. According to information given to Dr. Wilson, they were originated by a Japanese horticulturist who lived in Kurume more than a century ago. A popular variety of the Kurumes is Christmas Cheer: compact, Christmas red, hose-in-hose (semi-double), very popular.

Kaempferi Hybrids. The Kaempferi hybrids are practically evergreen in the South but may lose their leaves farther north. They are somewhat upright in growth, and although the flowers are smaller than those of the Indicas they are produced in considerable profusion. They appear to be just as hardy as the Kurumes. When the great beauty and dependability of this group become better known, many more of them will undoubtedly be planted in the South. They are especially recommended for the Upper South, Zone 7, where the winters are a bit too harsh for the Indicas. A well-known variety is Fedora (deep salmon rose).

Belgian Azaleas. The Belgian group of azaleas produces exceptionally large double and semidouble flowers in many brilliant colors and variations. The plants are rather slow growers and require a bit more attention than those of the other popular kinds. They are more tender to cold than the Indicas, but where proper protection can be given they make a marvelous showing. They are ideal for pot culture and are extensively planted for florists' trade. A popular variety in this group is Blushing Bride: double, blush pink, late.

Glendale Hybrids. The Glendales, which constitute one of the most valuable types of the azaleas grown in the South, were originated at Glenn Dale, Maryland, by my late friend Ben Y. Morrison, while he was in charge of the U.S. Plant Breeding Station there. After he left Glenn Dale and moved to the Mississippi Gulf Coast, he conducted a private breeding station at Pass Christian for many years. From there, he sent me twenty-three varieties of the Glendales to grow on test, all of which proved entirely satisfactory. In hardiness, they are somewhat between their parent plants, the Indicas and the Kurumes. My plants have never lost their flower buds even during the most severe winters, and I can recommend the Glendales for planting throughout the South. In the Meridian area they are evergreen, although not so heavily foliaged as most of the Indicas and Kurumes.

In my experience, all of the Glendale varieties are entirely worthwhile and are especially recommended for the Upper

South, where the winters get rather cold. A variety especially recommended is Fashion (orange-red).

AZALEA CULTURE

Winter Hardiness. Our winters in the South, while mild, are uncertain. In the North when winter comes the low temperatures hold until spring, but down here during winter we invariably have periods of a week or ten days, or sometimes considerably longer, when the weather is quite warm and springlike. If these warm periods are of long duration they stimulate the premature development of flower buds on the azaleas, only to have them injured by subsequent low temperatures. Many times freezes will leave no immediate indication of injury, but if later the buds are pinched open it will be found that the centers are brown, which is evidence of serious damage—enough, in fact, to prevent them from opening.

The conditions under which the azaleas are grown have much to do with their ability to stand hard cold. Plants given too much food and water, and those grown in full shade, produce wood that is less hardy than that on plants grown in sun and given a moderate amount of food and water. Tender, sappy growth will be killed back by a freeze that would do no damage to plants grown under proper conditions. This does not imply that plants should be permitted to go into winter lacking in moisture. Freezing is a drying process, and the plants should have adequate moisture at all times, especially during periods when they are subjected to low temperatures.

Since tender growth is more susceptible to winter injury than mature growth, it is not advisable to give feeding or other treatment which would stimulate the late development of new wood that would not have time to harden before cold arrives.

Small, young plants are more susceptible to winter injury than large established ones and should be given protection during periods of exceptionally low temperatures.

In many cases, hard cold will cause the bark on the canes to split. The plants may show no evidence of injury until weeks or months later, when the canes will begin to die. If plants are examined shortly after each freeze, many of the damaged branches may be saved by pulling the bark together, coating with grafting wax and wrapping with ordinary mending tape. If the split is not serious, the tape may be used without the wax. On several occasions, we have used this method and repaired with very good results. All canes damaged beyond repair should be neatly pruned out.

Soil. The soil for azaleas should be well filled with humus and must be **loose and friable.** The root system of the azalea is quite fibrous, and the soil must be sufficiently open and loose to allow full opportunity for development of these hairlike roots. If the soil is already moderately porous and friable, the only treatment necessary, perhaps, will be to incorporate liberal quantities of leaf mold or peat moss. In alkaline areas, however, better results will be obtained by removing the soil to a depth of some twelve inches and filling in with a soil prepared by mixing equal parts of garden loam and leaf mold or of garden loam and peat moss. Topsoil from a wooded area and half-rotted leaves are excellent for mixing with the soil, as these items not only add to the friability of the soil but to its acidity as well.

Both oak and cypress sawdust may be used very successfully in preparing soil for azaleas. Two parts soil and one part sawdust should give good results. The sawdust, which is acid in its reaction, decays slowly and tends to hold the soil open.

Azaleas belong to the family of ericaceous plants, and the soil for them must be not only friable and loose but **acid** as well. Acidity of soil is an essential; nothing will take its place.

The condition brought about by the lack of available acid in the soil is not difficult to diagnose. First, the leaves begin to yellow between the veins, with the veins remaining green; if the condition becomes more aggravated, the edges of the leaves may turn brown and die. Then the ends of the twigs die, and finally the entire plant fades out of the picture.

The degree of acidity of soil is usually expressed by the symbol "pH." Garden soils may be acid, neutral or alkaline. A pH of 7 is considered neutral, which implies that the soil is neither acid nor alkaline; if the pH runs above 7 the soil is alkaline; if the pH runs below 7 it is acid. A soil showing a pH of 9, let us say, would be too alkaline for most plant life; while one showing a pH of 4 would be too acid for all except a limited number of species. The precise degree of acidity for the best development of the different species of azaleas has not been determined, so far as is known; when further experimenting is done it will probably be found that some species require a soil of a higher acid content than others for their most satisfactory growth. It is said, however, that, as a family, azaleas should have a soil showing a pH of 4.5 to 6.5, and an analysis showing a range of 5 to 6 would be satisfying to the majority of them.

Before we can do much about bringing about the proper acid content of the soil, it would be well to make an analysis to determine the degree of acidity already present. Small test kits, adequate for the home gardener, may be purchased for a few dollars. Of course, many people grow azaleas without soil analysis, but the purchase of these little kits is one of the best investments any gardener can make.

Where the acid content is only slightly low, about 6 pH, for example, an annual heavy mulch of oak leaves or pine needles and the use of an azalea-camellia fertilizer would probably be sufficient to bring the degree of acidity down to standard requirements. If the pH is higher, it is customary to use one of the chemical agents.

Many times plants suffering from lack of acid may be temporarily sustained by spraying with a solution of one ounce of iron sulphate (copperas) to a gallon of water. In many cases the beneficial effect of the spray is evidenced by a better color of foliage in two or three days. A second application may be given in ten days if thought necessary. You may also water the plants with this same solution if they do not respond properly to spraying.

Aluminum sulphate, iron chelates and sulphur are also dependable acidifying agents.

If the trouble cannot be corrected by one of the remedies

suggested, and particularly if the leaves have a tendency to brown and die, you may have a drainage problem.

In applying the acidifying agents to the soil, it is usually best to pull the mulch away with a rake, scatter the acidifying material around the roots of the individual plants and wet down lightly, after which the mulch should be replaced. It should be understood that these acids are not plant foods and can in no way take the place of fertilizers.

Planting. Azaleas are among the easiest of all shrubs to transplant and may be moved very early or very late in the season if properly dug and kept well watered after the planting is done. They are easily moved while in bloom; in fact, that is when most of them are transplanted. Records of some of the large Gulf Coast nurserymen show that of all their annual sales approximately 90 percent are made while the plants are in bloom. There are several advantages of buying plants while in flower, one of which is that the purchaser can see exactly what he is buying. All too many times catalog descriptions disappoint us.

While the plants may be successfully moved while in bloom and the planting season may be extended well into spring, it should be added that, as with most shrubs, the ideal time for planting azaleas is early winter. This gives the plants time to establish themselves before the spring flowering season arrives; their roots start growing, so they will be in much better condition to go through the first summer and will require less attention than if they were planted late in the season.

Both the planting and culture of azaleas may be much more economically handled if they are planted in clumps or beds, and the color effects are always much better when used in this manner.

In planting individual plants, a hole at least two feet square should be made, even for small plants. Several inches of prepared soil should be placed in the bottom of the hole and packed down firmly before the plant is placed, in order to prevent its settling too much. Prepared soil should be used in filling in around the roots after the plant is placed in the hole. When planting in beds, remove the soil from the entire area down to about twelve inches. Fill in with about six or eight inches of prepared soil previously mentioned; place the plants and fill in between them with the soil mixture.

Azaleas should be so handled that, when the planting is completed and the soil has settled, the bed will be an inch or two higher than the surrounding surface. If drainage is a real problem, the bed may be raised several inches above the garden surface in order to provide proper drainage. Your particular location will have to determine these matters.

Cultivation. The soil around azaleas should never be broken with hoe, rake or spade as is so often done in the culture of other shrubs. As previously suggested, the roots of azaleas are fibrous and quite near the surface. Any breaking of the soil around the plants will invariably cause serious damage to the root system. If weeds of any kind appear, as they surely will, pull them out, but use no implements that will disturb the roots of the plants.

Mulches are positively essential in growing azaleas. There are several reasons why this is true. A good mulch does much to protect the roots during the hot, dry days of summer and fall; during winter, it protects the roots from freezes, retards evaporation and thereby conserves moisture. If made of acid-containing material, it will aid considerably in keeping the acid content of the soil up to standard requirements. It eliminates the need of cultivation by keeping the weeds down; and, finally, it will decay and add to the fertility of the soil.

As a rule azaleas do not require extra heavy fertilization. If they are properly planted and cared for, **one liberal feeding** right after the blooms have faded in spring will normally meet their annual food requirements. The special azalea-camellia plant food is recommended.

Azaleas require lots of **moisture**, but drainage must be good. The soil should be kept moist at all times, but not soggy. Newly set plants should be watered frequently to prevent them from drying out; they require more frequent watering during dry periods than most plants, and unless watched carefully may die out quickly before we realize they are in trouble. During the hot, dry weather of summer and fall, especially in areas where the rainfall is light, azaleas should be watered twice weekly. Watch the plants and water as often as there is evidence of a need of more moisture. During dry periods, spraying the foliage with a hose in the late afternoons, in addition to soaking the soil, will do much to revive the plants and restore vigor.

Flower buds of azaleas, in common with those of several other ornamentals, are formed during late summer and fall. It is particularly necessary that the plants be given ample moisture during this period. Lack of moisture during the period of bud development may result in a light crop of poor-quality buds or, in severe cases, a complete failure. These results may not be observed by the casual gardener until spring, when the plants fail to produce blooms. Many cases of failure of buds to open, attributed to freezes, are really due to lack of moisture during the fall months.

Pruning. Azaleas, as a whole, require little pruning. If general pruning is considered necessary, it should be given right after the flowers fade in the spring, in order to give ample time for the production of new wood for the following spring's flowers. Most of the varieties found in Southern gardens, if given room, will develop naturally into bushy, compact plants which carry the branches well down to the soil. A few, however, like William Bull, Elegans and the Kaempferi hybrids, are rather upright growers with an open development. Some of these varieties, however, will eventually fill in considerably and become more compact as they grow older. The long, slender canes which run up without branching should be cut back not later than early summer.

Sun and Shade. Azaleas, in common with practically all other plants found in Southern gardens, should have a certain amount of sunlight for their best development. Plants grown in sun make shorter annual growths, the plants become more compact in development, the wood is tougher and more hardy to winter cold and the crops of flower buds are heavier, provided the plants get sufficient moisture as well as full sunlight. But unless plants grown in full sunlight are well established, the matter of supplying sufficient moisture requires a great deal of effort and entails considerable thought and attention, especially during the dry periods of late summer and fall. Young plants find the direct rays of our midsummer sun even more trying than older ones and should be given some protection.

Azaleas will do well in full shade, however, if the light is good; even on the north side of low buildings, where the sun rarely ever strikes them, they grow well and bloom profusely.

Insects and Diseases. The **azalea lace bug** is probably the most serious insect pest with which the azalea grower has to deal. Damage is caused by both nymphs and adults that suck the juices from the undersides of the leaves, causing a grayish, splotched or blanched appearance. The foliage of badly infested plants has the appearance of being mildewed and may have a yellowish tint. The undersides of the leaves evidence a brownish-black varnishlike excrement, and the skins of the molts also adhere to the under surfaces of the foliage. In cases of severe infestation, the plants are greatly devitalized, practically stop growing and take on a stunted appearance.

The adult lace bug is about an eighth of an inch in length, with lacelike wings with brown markings. The eggs are deposited within the tissues of the undersides of the leaves and incubate in about three weeks.

Control is effected by the use of oil-base sprays, either miscible oil, oil emulsion or prepared sprays, but they are more effective if derris powder or nicotine sulphate is added. Dependable prepared sprays may be obtained at practically all seed stores; these should be used according to directions on the package (see Chapter 28).

Mites, commonly known as red spiders, sometimes become a major pest, especially during hot, dry weather. They feed on both the under and upper surfaces of the leaves, sucking vital plant juices, causing the leaves to turn reddish brown. Adult females may be almost black, but the men of the family and the children are light red. Oil sprays recommended for lace bugs should check mites.

For several years the **azalea bloom blight** was the most dreaded of all azalea diseases. It is indicated by wilting of the blooms, much as if scalding water had been poured over them. It spreads rapidly, and blooms from entire plantings may be destroyed in a few days. Your seed store will probably have dependable remedies.

Azalea gall is a disease characterized by thickened, fleshy growths in the leaves, flowers and twigs, which are usually gall-like. Its appearance is usually in spring, during the rainy season. The galls should be cut out and the plants sprayed with a good fungicide.

RHODODENDRONS IN THE MIDDLE SOUTH

As our scientific knowledge of horticulture widens and more extensive experiments are made, we learn that many genera and species of plants which we once thought could not be grown in certain areas will do very well there if their basic needs are met. Japonica camellias, for example, are being grown much farther north than they were two decades ago, and peonies seem to be moving considerably farther south. Most of us are familiar with the marvelous rhododendrons which cover much of the mountainous sections of Tennessee, Virginia and North Carolina and the extreme northwest sections of this country, but we have been told repeatedly that they will not thrive in the Middle or Deep South.

Some of my neighbors here in the Meridian area have been growing lovely rhododendrons for several years, and I am sure one can find plants in other sections of the Middle and Deep South. In an article written by Arthur I. Coyle, an eminent horticulturist of Houston, Texas, and published in a recent *Newsletter* of the Louisiana Society for Horticultural Research, the author outlined his success in growing these plants in his home city. He is growing more than a hundred types in his home gardens.

With Mr. Coyle's permission, I am basing most of my comments here on his interesting paper, which was read before the Gulf Coast Botanical Society meeting in Houston. Mr. Coyle tells us that this genus of plants contains about a thousand species, including our popular azalea series.

Some rhododendrons, we are told, must be grown in a climate with cool summers and mild winters, such as exist in the extreme northwest portion of this country, as well as in the British Isles. But there are many species that will tolerate extremely cold winters, and a very select group will tolerate both cold winters and hot summers. It is from this group that Middle South gardeners will have to make their selections.

"We do not know," writes Mr. Coyle, "of any rhododendrons other than those of the azalea series which will do well in the full Texas sun." But he adds that several species and varieties will thrive in Houston if given partial shade and a few other special basic needs. What would apply to Houston should apply to practically all of the Middle South.

Mr. Coyle states four basic requirements for growing rhododendrons in a hot climate: (1) Have sufficient shade available to protect the plants from the direct rays of the sun, especially in the afternoon. (2) Have water available; it should not be too high above the neutral pH point. (3) A light friable soil is a must; it should be between 4 and 5 pH for most rhododendrons grown in the hot areas. If an acid soil is not a natural occurrence, the planting area can be made acid with German peat moss and iron sulphate. (Never use aluminum sulphate, because the excess aluminum ions that would be available under acid conditions would kill the rhododendrons.) (4) Observe soil culture strictly. A mixture of half peat moss and half perlite is suggested for Texas soil, and that should work very well in this area. If the perlite is not easily available, you could use a mixture that is considered satisfactory for azaleas.

It is suggested that, before planting, you wash off much of the earth in the ball around the roots with the hose to expose several inches of the roots, so they will have ready access to the new growing medium used for filling in around the plant.

Mr. Coyle emphasizes the importance of good drainage. He suggests that no hole be dug in planting, but that the area be leveled off, the plant placed on a layer of gravel and the soil mixture used to fill around it. When the planting is finished, the rhododendron should be sitting on a raised bed where the drainage is perfect.

Mr. Coyle states that his selection of rhododendrons for growing in this part of the South was originally based on the theory that cold tolerance and heat tolerance went hand in hand, but that he has since learned that even some of the more tender ones will withstand high temperatures. Disease resistance, he says, has proved to be as important a factor as heat resistance in growing these plants in hot areas. Drainage is another important factor.

The following medium-hardy rhododendrons have done well for Mr. Coyle and should grow in this area if given the proper cultural attention: Alba Elegans, apple-blossom pink; *R. catawbiense albus,* white; English Roseum, light pink; Roseum Elegans, pink; Roseum Superbum, rose; *R. catawbiense grandiflorum,* lilac rose; Nova Zambla, red; and American, dark red. The following varieties, considered very winter hardy, have also done well in Houston: Loder's white; Jean Marie deMontague, red; Margaret Dubb, apricot; Mrs. T. M. Lowkinsky, blush red; Marinus Koster, deep pink; Vulcan, deep red; and Betty Warmald, pink.

Summing up the situation, I would suggest we should always plant rhododendrons in partial to full shade. The best plants in Meridian are grown on the north sides of buildings, in full shade but in good light; use about the same soil mixture you would for azaleas; provide plenty of moisture, but be sure, definitely sure, that the drainage is not only good but perfect.

If Mr. Coyle can grow rhododendrons successfully in Houston, we should be able to grow them in almost any part of the Middle South.

20

Camellias

The mere sight of old camellia trees in the fullness of their exotic bloom tends not only to stop Time in his ruthless, headlong flight but to turn him back for a century or more to a period when life in the South was rich, real and full. Gardens where old camellias are grown have a distinctive, aristocratic air, the flavor of genuine good taste, culture, refinement and fine living. These shrubs give the horticultural planting a distinctive atmosphere not supplied by any other ornamental plant.

The camellia is named for George Kamel, 1661–1706 (in Latin, Camellus), a Moravian Jesuit who supposedly traveled widely in Asia in the seventeenth century. While numerous species may be found in tropical and subtropical sections of Asia, our modern camellias can no doubt be traced to plants brought from China to Europe over a period of years beginning about the year 1739.

The descriptive name "japonica" attached to the best known of the species indicates that it came from Japan, but horticultural names are many times misleading. No positive evidence that the species actually originated in Japan seems to be available; it could as easily have been China or Korea.

It is not known just when or how the camellia was introduced in our Southern home grounds, but we do know that travelers in the early years of the settlement of the South brought plants

152

with them from the "old country," and in those early years specimens of *Camellia japonica* were found in the vicinity of Charleston, Augusta, Pensacola, Mobile, New Orleans, Natchez and other old centers of wealth and culture. The records indicate that long before the Civil War there were more than a hundred varieties of camellias grown in the Magnolia Gardens near Charleston, and no doubt there were many other old plantings in the South which contained a considerable number of varieties during this period.

Owing to the unusually long life of the camellia, it should be noted that he who plants it is not planting for today alone but for generations to come. His children may live to bless the person who plants a camellia.

SPECIES OF CAMELLIAS

While there are several species of camellias, most of those grown in the South are either *C. japonica* or *C. sasanqua*, with the first greatly in the majority. *Camellia japonica*, the "japonica" of our grandmothers' gardens, is a relatively tall shrub with large, leathery dark-green leaves, unusually handsome in appearance, with a flowering season which extends, according to variety, from fall until spring.

Some varieties, particularly the very desirable Arejishi, Daikagura and High Hat, are normally in bloom by mid-October; Arejishi sometimes blooms as early as July, but the main flowering season for the great majority of the "camellia belt" is from the middle of January to the middle of March.

C. sasanqua is an early bloomer of more recent introduction; it is a plant of many good qualities. In many areas it is found in bloom by the middle of October and should be in full bloom in most areas by the middle of November. Blooming at a time when there is little color in the shrub borders, these fall-flowering camellias are especially desirable. They are certainly worthy of much heavier planting throughout the South.

In recent years much interest has been shown in other species of camellias, particularly *C. reticulata*, which has been popular in England for many years. Many fine specimens of this species are found on our West Coast.

As with other plants, the high price of the camellia does not always indicate superior qualities. In some cases scarcity and difficulty in propagation may result in a variety of ordinary merit being quite high in price. The new and rare varieties are usually higher in price.

If at all practicable, visit the nursery and see the plants in bloom; then make selections according to your own good taste and judgment. You will know exactly what you are getting for your money, and there will be far less room for disappointment when another flowering season rolls around.

One of the best methods of acquainting ourselves with the different varieties is to attend at least a few of the various camellia shows, where one may find blooms of all the newer and most popular varieties. It is the best opportunity to see and compare the latest introductions.

CAMELLIA CULTURE

Established camellia plants will usually stand considerable cold; even in the latitude of Tyler, Little Rock, Memphis, Birmingham and Atlanta, east to the Atlantic coast and as far north as the Norfolk area, old plants are rarely severely damaged. Camellias relish a cool, moist climate and bloom best in a temperature of about 50 degrees. But inasmuch as opening buds and flowers are rather easily injured by freezes, some consideration should be given this phase of their culture when the planting is made.

Tender wood, of course, is much more easily damaged by cold than mature wood. Late feeding tends to keep the plants growing into late fall and early winter, producing new wood that does not have sufficient time to harden before winter cold arrives. For this reason, feeding with nitrogenous fertilizer later than early summer is not recommended.

In the colder areas, many growers give preference to the very early and very late varieties. The very early ones usually furnish a fair crop of blooms before severe winter weather arrives; the very late ones hold their buds tight throughout the winter and do not make an effort to bloom until the coldest of the winter is past.

Soil. While most good garden soils will grow camellias, one that is deep, rich, filled with a liberal content of humus and somewhat acid is best. Most of our soils are made more to the liking of these shrubs by mixing in a generous quantity of leaf mold or commercial humus of some kind. A formula consisting of two parts garden loam, one part leaf mold, one part peat moss and one part dehydrated manure (cow or sheep) should be very satisfactory. If leaf mold is not available, use two parts peat. Care should be used to see that the different elements are well mixed.

The root system of the camellia is not as fibrous as that of the azalea, nor are the plants quite so shallow-rooted, and for these reasons they may be grown in soils where azaleas would not thrive. And while camellias require an acid soil, it need not be quite so acid as for azaleas. A soil running lightly to the acid side, anywhere from 5.5 to 6.5 pH, should satisfy them. If camellias are properly planted, mulched annually with peat, oak leaves or pine needles and fed with azalea-camellia plant food, additional acid in chemical form will hardly be necessary.

Planting. While camellias are not quite as easily transplanted as azaleas, if properly handled they may be transplanted with the assurance that they will grow. Transplanting is usually done during the dormant season, which normally runs from late fall to early spring. Except in the case of very small plants, they are always handled balled and burlapped, unless, of course, they are in containers.

Camellias are planted individually, and it is necessary to dig a separate hole for each plant. Thought also must be given to the matter of drainage. It is usually the safest plan to dig the hole deep enough that four to six inches of gravel, crushed stone or similar material can be placed in the bottom before the plant-

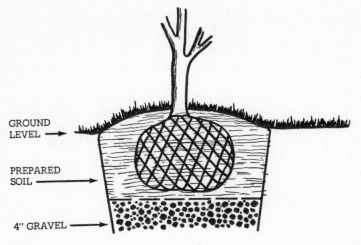

GROUND
LEVEL →

PREPARED
SOIL →

4" GRAVEL →

Be careful not to plant camellias too deep. If doubtful about the
drainage, raise the plant slightly.

ing is done. In very low areas, as in the vicinity of New Orleans,
the difficulty may be met by planting on raised beds or mounds.

After good drainage has been provided, the hole should be
deep enough that at least four inches of prepared soil can
be placed in the bottom before the plant is set, and it should be
wide enough that at least six inches of soil can be placed between
the ball containing the roots and the walls of the hole.

To prevent undue settling, the soil in the bottom of the hole
should be firmly packed before the plant is placed. Planted in
normally well-drained soil, the plant should be slightly higher
than it grew in the nursery when the job is finished and the
earth settled.

The plant should be so handled that the ball of earth is not
broken; even cracking the ball will result in breaking many of
the small feeder roots and injuring the plant.

Many progressive nurserymen now grow their camellias in
containers, which method of handling has some definite advantages. Plants grown in pots or cans may be planted at any season
of the year with their entire root system intact. When buying

canned plants, be sure to have the seller slit the container to facilitate removal of the plant.

After a planting of camellias has been made, regardless of how handled, each plant should be well watered.

Cultivation. While camellias are not so shallow-rooted as azaleas, cultivation of the soil around these plants should be discouraged, as digging to any considerable depth will surely injure the root system. A heavy annual **mulch** is definitely recommended. If a good mulch is kept around the plants, all cultivation may be eliminated. Any stray weeds coming through the mulch may be readily pulled out. Mulches may be of any one of several materials: leaves, pine needles, lawn clippings, oak or cypress sawdust, peat or other commercial humus. Oak leaves, pine needles and peat and the sawdusts mentioned are especially recommended because of their acid content. Pine needles make an excellent mulch and are much neater than leaves.

Sun and Shade. Most of us have seen fine old camellias growing in full sun, and we have also seen them growing in full shade, but neither situation is considered ideal. In full sun the growth is usually quite slow and it is more difficult to maintain adequate moisture at the roots, but the plants fill in much better and give a stocky development and the crop of flower buds is heavy as a rule. The summer sun is rather trying on the foliage of even old well-established plants. Where the sun's rays fall directly on the plants, there is usually evidence of sun scald. This condition is indicated by brown spots on the leaves, ranging from very small ones up to the size of a quarter dollar or larger.

Camellias should never be placed in a position where they will be exposed to full sun while frozen. The full sun striking a plant covered with ice will usually cause serious damage to the foliage and may even kill back the branches.

Camellias will stand considerable shade, as much, perhaps, as any of the broad-leaf evergreens commonly grown in our gardens. In fact, they will grow and bloom well in full shade, if there is high overhead light, or in locations where the sun strikes them for only a few hours daily, as on the north sides of buildings. In shady locations, the quality of both foliage and bloom is improved, but if the shade is too dense and the light poor, the wood is inclined to be soft, the plants are less stocky and there may be fewer flower buds.

The ideal condition with reference to sun and shade is somewhat similar to that suggested for azaleas. A situation under or near trees, where there is plenty of light but where the rays of the sun are broken by the foliage overhead, should be ideal for growing camellias. Commercially, most young plants are grown in lath houses, with laths alternately spaced, which gives the plants adequate protection.

Watering. Camellias require much moisture in the soil for their best growth and general development, but the drainage must be good. In most sections of the South the rainfall is ample from early winter until late spring, but during the summer and fall months the plants, especially young ones and those not thoroughly established, will require artificial watering. When water is applied, the ground should be soaked to a great depth. The roots go much deeper than those of azaleas and more water will be needed to reach the deepest ones. Remove the nozzle from the hose and let the water run until you are definitely sure that it has reached the deepest roots. Sprinkling the foliage in the late afternoons, as suggested for azaleas, will greatly help the plants during extremely hot, dry periods, but sprinkling must be in addition to the water applied at the roots, not in lieu of it.

Dropping of Buds. Dropping of buds is usually caused by improper culture or growing conditions. Of course, a freeze after the buds have begun to expand will result in some loss, but when buds drop excessively without any apparent cause the real trouble usually goes back to poor gardening.

Poor drainage and planting too deeply may easily result in bud dropping. Another common cause is lack of moisture in late summer and fall when the buds are developing; this is probably responsible for more cases of buds shedding than anything else.

Some varieties simply put on more buds than can be supported by the vitality of the plant, and some may drop before opening. Use judgment and remove some of the buds if the crop appears to be too heavy.

Feeding. Camellias are rather heavy feeders and normally should be fed twice each year, first in the spring, about the time the plants have finished flowering, with a second application in June. Most seed stores in the Deep South now carry dependable ready-mixed azalea-camellia fertilizers which are very satisfactory. If these special plant foods are not available, one of the balanced garden fertilizers may be used; one of the high-test products mixed half and half with cottonseed meal will also give good results.

For individual plants the quantity of food to use would vary with the size of the plant, of course, but for a very small one a heaping tablespoonful of azalea-camellia plant food would probably suffice; for a larger plant, any amount up to a teacupful would be in order.

We may usually determine from the general appearance of a plant if it is in need of plant food, and if such a condition occurs, the applications should be increased. In feeding, the mulch should be pulled away, the fertilizer scattered around the plant and the mulch replaced, after which the plant should be watered.

Insects and Diseases. While camellias are not attacked by many kinds of insect enemies, there are several types of scale that may prove disastrous in a very short time. Even large plants may be killed by tea scale in a single season. The leaves of heavily infested plants may show splotches of yellow, while the insects in various stages of development may be found on the undersides of the leaves. One of the white oil or miscible oil sprays, or any one of the several summer scale sprays, when properly used, should check these insects after a few applications. These sprays may be found at practically all seed stores and, if used according to directions on the package, are usually both safe and effective.

Because of the importance of scale, plants should be examined occasionally to determine if any infestation has begun; if found, immediate steps should be taken to check the insects. The most effective spray schedule consists of one application in the spring with a second in from four to six weeks. In cases of heavy infestation, a final clean-up spray should be given in September.

Oil sprays should not be applied in winter; neither should they be applied when the temperature is above 90 degrees. In spraying, turn the nozzle upward so as to direct the solution to the undersides of the leaves; that is where the insects live and raise their families. If we are not careful to cover the undersides of the leaves completely, many of the little scale children will escape, only to give us serious trouble a little later, for they soon grow to adult size and start families of their own.

Camellias are attacked by several diseases, but only the most important ones will be considered here. Some are rare and not often encountered, while others are of little consequence. We will comment only on those about which it is thought the average gardener should be informed.

There seems to be considerable confusion over the disease called **dieback,** as the term is loosely applied to several forms of camellia ailments. True or typical dieback is evidenced by the dying of an entire twig at once, without previous indications of trouble in that area. In new growths, the twigs wilt and droop, and unless remedial measures are taken the disease may extend down the twig to the next larger branch and continue its disastrous work. The most effective control measures known at this time seem to be judicial pruning to remove all diseased twigs and branches, followed by sprayings with a good fungicide. Prunings should be burned.

Leaf Spot, a fungus disease, is evidenced by dark brown spots of various sizes on the leaves and as a rule does not greatly damage the plants. Spraying with any dependable fungicide is recommended.

Camellia blossom blight, which has given some trouble on the West Coast for several years, has been found in some sections of the South. It is indicated by wet dark-brown discolorations on the flower petals. The disease begins with a small toadstool about one-half inch in diameter which releases its spores into the air. Under favorable conditions they lodge on the flower and begin their dirty work. Spraying the ground under and near the plants every two weeks with some good fungicide is said to keep the disease down.

21

Bulbs

For sheer beauty, bulbs and bulbous plants hold a leading place among garden flowers. The spring-flowering bulbs come into bloom before winter is gone, when flowers are none too plentiful even here in the South, and supply color when it is much needed. They are satisfactory for cutting and bedding, and their period of bloom extends over a long season.

The characteristic of these plants which probably appeals most to the amateur is their ease of culture. While a few of the lilies are a bit fastidious and require a little special care, most of the bulbs will shift for themselves as well as any other flowers in the garden. Many of them, if planted in good soil, can be left undisturbed for several years. Most will respond equally well in full sun or partial shade, and a few will thrive in full shade. Planted in beds, they give masses of striking color. Many are desirable as border plants, others are excellent material for cutting and still others are most desirable for planting among the shrubs of the foundation and in the shrub borders.

The early-flowering bulbs should appeal strongly to the gardener who has only a small area at his command and who must resort to intensive gardening in order to have something in bloom the year through. They can always be followed by annuals, and thus the blooming season is carried through the year.

162

There seems to be general confusion about the meaning of the word "bulb." The term is often used to refer to many plants that are not bulbs at all. A true bulb can be identified by the layers of scales which compose it; lilies and onions are good examples. A corm is composed of woody fibers, such as the gladiolus, for instance. A rhizome is a fibrous root, as found in the bearded iris. A tuber is an enlarged root, as in the dahlia or sweet potato. Remember, it is not a bulb unless it is composed of scales.

BULB CULTURE

Soil. Soil requirements for bulbs and bulbous plants are very much the same. The soil should be deep and exceptionally loamy, and the drainage must be good. If the soil is inclined to be stiff, add sand or some form of humus. Two parts of ordinary garden soil with one part each of peat moss and leaf mold give a soil that will satisfy most of the bulbs. If you cannot get leaf mold, use commercial humus. Since most of the bulbs are ordinarily left undisturbed for several years and it is not practical to renew the beds annually, it is very important to get the soil in a highly congenial condition before planting.

Fertilizer. If you plant the bulbs in a bed, spade the soil to a depth of ten to twelve inches and mix your fertilizer well with the soil. Fresh animal manure is very injurious to most bulbs and should never be used. However, manure that is thoroughly decomposed or dehydrated and thoroughly mixed with the soil is a satisfactory plant food for many of the bulbs and bulbous plants. If you have any doubt about the manure being in proper condition, leave it out and use commercial plant food instead. A commercial food analyzing about 5-10-10, used at the rate of two pounds to a hundred square feet of bed, should give good results. For bulbs grown in rows, two pounds to a hundred feet of row is about right.

Bone meal, because of its slow action, is a safe fertilizer for all bulbs, and there is little danger of overfertilizing with it. You can

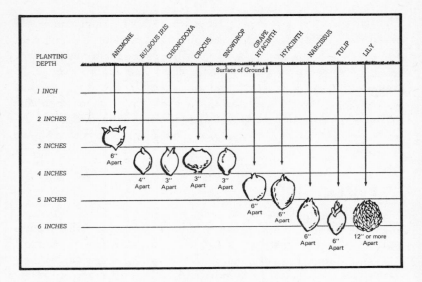

Chart showing proper depth for planting bulbs.

use it at the rate of three to four pounds to a hundred square feet of bed with perfect safety.

Planting. When you plant large bulbs—tulips, narcissi, hyacinths and lilies—in any considerable quantity, it is usually better to remove all of the soil from the entire bed, leaving the floor practically level. Then place two or three inches of good topsoil or enriched soil in the bottom of the bed, and on this spread about a half inch of sand, if it is available. Place all of the bulbs on this cushion of sand before filling in the bed.

With this method, all the bulbs are planted at a uniform depth. If planted at irregular depths, all the bulbs do not come into bloom at the same time; the shallowly planted ones bloom first. If you plant them individually, place a little sand under each bulb, unless the soil is exceptionally loose.

Daffodils and hyacinths should be covered to a depth of from two to six inches, depending on the size of the bulbs and the character of the soil. The larger bulbs should go deeper than the smaller ones, and they should not be planted as deep in stiff soils as in loose soils. About two inches of soil is satisfactory for the minor bulbs. (The depths suggested here indicate the amount of soil over the crowns of the bulbs.)

Drainage. All the bulbs mentioned require good drainage. If the natural drainage is not satisfactory, provide artificial drainage. Most bulbs will soon decay if you permit the soil to become soggy for lengthy periods. There are a few species that will grow in moist places, but these are rarely of general garden culture.

BULB VARIETIES

Amaryllis. The hybrid amaryllis, now available in various color combinations, is one of the most showy bulbs and should certainly be more generally planted. Through the azalea belt it can be grown outdoors. With only a good protection of straw it can be carried safely through temperatures several degrees below freezing. Soil requirements are about the same as for other bulbs, but this plant prefers a soil that is a little on the acid side. The bulbs require practically no attention, multiply rapidly, and are gorgeous when they are in bloom. Most of us would do well to plant more of them.

Hyacinths. The various terms used to list hyacinths in some catalogs are often confusing to people not well versed in gardening. The terms "Exhibition," "Bedding" and "Dutch Roman" may all refer to the same type of bulbs but to different sizes. Exhibition hyacinths are the largest size and usually measure 2½ inches or more in diameter. They are especially fine for forcing. Bedding hyacinths are smaller and are used for general garden planting. They should run about 2¼ inches in diameter. The Dutch Roman, sometimes called Miniatures, are still smaller. These smaller bulbs are satisfactory for bedding but cannot be expected to force satisfactorily.

"French Roman" or "French" hyacinths, which are supposedly grown in France, are of a distinctly different form. The flower spikes are smaller, and the flowers are more loosely spaced on the stems. But each well-grown bulb can be expected to produce several spikes of bloom. Hyacinths prefer a sunny location with very good drainage.

Daffodils. In recent years the terms "daffodil" and "narcissus" have come to be considered synonymous. Each term is meant to include the entire family of plants. "Daffodil" is considered the English equivalent of the Latin genus *Narcissus.*

Although the daffodil is one of our oldest flowers, it does not seem to have reached the heights of esteem that some far less meritorious flowers of the garden have. However, recent introductions are increasing interest in these flowers. The present trend seems to be toward pink and red trumpets.

In my experience the varieties with medium-sized flowers do better in the Middle and Lower South than those with huge flowers. As with tulips, our warm climate seems to cause the large bulbs to split up.

We Americans do not seem to find the time to do things as thoroughly as the English, and I am inclined to believe that the popularity of the daffodil in this country has been retarded by the intricate classifications adopted by the Royal Horticultural Society of England in 1908 and generally accepted by the trade in this country. Its eleven divisions are:

1. Trumpet. Trumpet or crown as long or longer than the perianth segments. Example: Alasnam.

2. Incomparabilis. Cup or crown not less than one third, but less than equal the length of the segments. Example: Croesus.

3. Barri. Cup or crown less than one third the length of the perianth segments. Example: Mrs. Barclay.

4. Leedsi. Perianth white and cup or crown white, cream or pale citron, sometimes tinged with pink or apricot. Example: Silver Star.

5. Triandrus. *N. triandrus* and its hybrids. Example: Moonshine.

6. Cyclamineus. *N. cyclamineus* and its hybrids. Example: February Gold.

7. Jonquilla. *N. jonquilla* and its hybrids. Example: Camper-nelle.

8. Tazetta. *N. tazetta* and its hybrids. Example: Laurens Koster.

9. Poet. Example: Snow King.

10. Doubles. Example: Mary Copeland.

11. Various. Includes *N. bulbocodium, N. cyclamineus, N. juncifolius* and *N. viridiflora,* among others.

One of the most effective uses of daffodils is to naturalize them along the margins of wooded areas and plant them in masses on sections of the lawn. When they are grown on the lawn, however, remember that the foliage of the bulbs should never be cut until it has turned yellow. Removal of the foliage while it is still green results in devitalized bulbs which may not flower the following spring.

September and October are good months in which to plant daffodils throughout the South.

Tulips. Although tulips may not be so satisfactory in the Lower South, they make a splendid showing in the Middle and Upper South. New uses are being found for them each season. They are no longer confined to geometrically designed beds in the front lawn but are now being used with pleasing effects in naturalistic beds along the shrubbery borders and in clumps about the foundation walls. There is no better use for these colorful bulbs than for planting in clumps of a dozen or more in little nooks along the foundation planting and in other positions where they have a background of shrubs.

Many gardeners in the South now treat tulips as an annual crop, discarding the bulbs after they have bloomed. If you do not plan to save the bulbs, they need be planted only about four inches deep. If, on the other hand, you plan to try carrying them over for another crop, you had better plant ten to twelve inches deep. Deep planting discourages splitting of the bulbs.

Minor Bulbs. When we speak of bulbs, most of us think only of daffodils, tulips, hyacinths and lilies; we fail to give due

thought to the large family of minor bulbs. Most of these little
bulbs come into bloom in the South before winter is quite over.
They are very good material for naturalizing along wooded
margins or for beds and clumps along the shrubbery borders.
They are an entirely worthwhile group, and most of us in the
South have failed to use them to their full value.

The **crocus**, one of the earliest to flower, is especially good for
naturalizing. It can be left undisturbed for a number of years.
About the time the crocuses are in flower, **chionodoxa** also comes
into bloom. Planting of these little bulbs will give a display of
unusual beauty and interest. The flowers are produced on dwarf
spikes, sometimes a dozen or more to the spike.

Under small trees and along the hedges and borders are delightful places for the little **snowdrop** (galanthus) and **snowflake**
(leucojum). They are among the very first to open in the spring
and are always a joy to see. Like the chionodoxa, they seem to
resent being disturbed and are happier when left in the same
position for years.

If there is a spot about your grounds that duplicates a woodland nook, particularly in moisture and shade, the **fritillarias and
erythroniums** should thrive there. The peculiar bell-shaped flowers of the fritillarias are quite attractive and interesting. The
erythroniums produce dainty, lily-shaped flowers in spring, which
run in delicate shades of white, pink, cream and yellow to rose.
The rich and mottled foliage greatly enhances their beauty.

Another interesting spring-flowering bulb of the minor group
is the **grape hyacinth,** or muscari, which produces purple grape-
like flowers on six-inch stems. **Winter aconite** and **scilla** are also
worthwhile. These can be fittingly planted with chionodoxas,
snowdrops and snowflakes.

Miscellaneous. The **anemone** and its cousin, the **ranunculus,**
are not true bulbs, but I mention them here because so many
gardeners think of them as belonging to the bulb family. You will
find the anemones in a wide variety of colors. They are valuable
for both pots and garden planting. St. Brigid, a semidouble
variety, is especially desirable. Ranunculi are of very easy culture

and make a grand showing in the spring. Plant both anemones and ranunculi in the fall.

The **summer hyacinth** (*Galtonia candicans*), a native of South Africa, is very satisfactory for outdoor planting in the South. Its stately stalks, four to five feet high, bear great numbers of pure white, bell-shaped flowers. It is an interesting summer subject. **Peruvian daffodils** (ismenes), **tiger flowers** (*Tigridia pavonia*), **tuberous begonias** and **montbretias** are other summer-flowering plants you shouldn't overlook when you make your planting plans.

Then, of course, all Southern gardens should have liberal plantings of alstroemeria, crinum, caladium, ornithogalum and the various zephyranthes. The pink rain lily, *Zephyranthes rosea*, is one of the loveliest of all bulbous plants. It is very easily grown and has large, lilylike, rose-colored flowers. Its interesting habit of sending up quantities of bloom spikes after each summer rain or heavy watering from the hose adds to its charm.

In the warmer sections of the South, the calla lily, zantedeschia, is becoming a popular garden plant. It requires a light soil, heavy proportions of humus, partial shade and considerable moisture. *Z. elliottiana* is a yellow form. Callas should be watered sparingly until growth begins, then more heavily. Too much water before the leaves start growth may cause decay of the bulbs.

22

Roses

TYPES OF ROSES

Bush Roses. Of the bush roses grown in the South, the hybrid teas constitute by far the major group. They were produced by crossing the tender teas with the old hybrid perpetuals. This group possesses much of the hardiness of the hybrid perpetuals but has the continuous blooming qualities of the teas. The Cochets are good examples of the teas, while the hybrid teas may be represented by Americana, Charlotte Armstrong, Granada, Peace and many others.

The hybrid teas may be subdivided into several groups, one of which is the grandifloras. This group is vigorous growing and includes some of the country's most popular roses. They have large flowers after the fashion of the hybrid teas, but there is a tendency of the flowers to occur in clusters. Popular representatives of the grandiflora group include John S. Armstrong, Queen Elizabeth and Pink Parfait.

There is still another group called floribundas. This is a term applied to the large-flowered polyanthus, and they are ideal for bedding or planting in situations where mass color effect is desired. Popular representatives of the floribundas include Angel Face, Apricot Nectar, Betty Prior and Cecile Brunner.

There are a number of dwarfish varieties of this type, including the popular China Doll, Pigmy Gold and Pigmy Red, that are excellent for use along borders, walks and driveways. These small compact plants usually stay within bounds and are easily cared for.

A few years ago a small-flowered group of roses called poly-anthus was very popular. They were dwarfish in growth but produced immense heads of flowers through a long season. The catalogs seem to be discontinuing the listing of this type but have included many of the most popular ones in the floribunda group.

Climbing Roses. Few other climbing plants can approach in beauty and charm a climbing rose in full bloom. For covering fences (both old and new), stumps, outhouses of various kinds, pergolas and entrances, they can hardly be equaled.

Climbing roses may be classed as either tender or hardy. The hardy climbers, of which we may mention the old Dr. W. Van Fleet, Mary Wallace, Thor and Dr. J. H. Nicholas, bloom only in the spring and give a gorgeous mass of color at that time. The tender climbers, like Columbia, Climbing Spartan, Coral Satin and Climbing Crimson Glory give a great burst of bloom in the spring and with proper care and culture should give continuous bloom throughout the summer and fall. Some of them are grown to the height of only six or eight feet, while others—Dr. Van Fleet, for example—may be permitted to ramble all over the garage.

Climbing roses differ widely in their cultural requirements and character of growth. That we may better understand them, let us divide the climbers further into two general groups: ramblers and true climbers.

The **ramblers,** which are usually identified by their clusters of small flowers, renew themselves by sending up new shoots from the ground each spring. They should be cut well back to the earth each spring after they have flowered, removing the old canes and leaving only the strong vigorous new growth.

In the class of **true climbers** we place those roses which begin their growth each spring at the terminals of last year's canes.

They are usually vigorous growers and include the tender plants such as Climbing Columbia, Climbing Talisman and Climbing Peace and the hardy ones such as Dr. Van Fleet, Silver Moon, Doubloons and Thor.

The true climbers will not require any heavy pruning except for cleaning out dead and diseased wood. If, however, the climbers are getting out of bounds, no harm will be done if they are cut back rather severely.

Many of us are inclined to neglect our climbing roses and forget to feed and water them. If they are given plenty of water, and food three or four times during the season, we will have much healthier plants and definitely more and better flowers.

GROWING ROSES IN THE SOUTH

Roses may be planted any time from late fall to spring in the South, but early planting is preferred. In most sections, roses will reach a state of dormancy that will justify moving them by early November—and November and December are regarded as the best planting months in most areas.

In our warm climate, root development on many plants starts very early, long before there is any evidence of leaf bud growth. Early planting gives time for root development before leaf growth starts. However, in the Upper South many growers prefer to wait until February to plant.

Where to Plant. While the location of the beds should be sunny, it is not necessary that they be in full sun; a location that will give sun for five or six hours in the morning, with protection from the afternoon sun, would probably be better. Some experiments have been made in growing roses in lath houses, with laths alternately spaced, and the results have been highly satisfactory. Under such treatment the plants appear more vigorous, and both foliage and blooms are of high quality.

The beds should not be placed under or near shallow-rooted trees, which will rob the roses of food and moisture. If roses must be grown where the earth is filled with tiny tree roots, considerable work will be necessary to supply sufficient food and moisture to care adequately for the roses after the trees have taken their toll.

Soil. It has been my experience that any good soil will grow roses. A soil that is ideal for the average farm or vegetable crop should also grow good roses. Such a soil, of course, would be quite fertile, deep and well drained. In most locations in the South drainage is not a problem, but where it is poor, some remedial measures should be taken. Many times the difficulty can be met by raising the bed an inch or two above the surrounding surface; if the situation is really bad, underground tile may be laid under the bed.

If the soil is rather stiff, coarse sand, commercial humus or leaf mold (preferably the last two) may be worked in before the planting is made. If the soil is unusually sandy, a little clay or leaf mold or both, thoroughly mixed with the soil, will help. Should the location selected be hard clay or extremely sandy, it may be necessary to remove the earth from the entire area of the bed, to a depth of about fifteen to eighteen inches, and fill in with a good garden soil.

Much has been written in recent years about the relation of soil acidity to rose growing. Many experiments seem to indicate that soil showing an analysis slightly below neutral—between 6 and 7 pH—is most desirable. In my own experience, soils showing an analysis of approximately neutral (7 pH) will grow roses satisfactorily if other conditions are favorable.

Lack of acid is usually evidenced by yellowing of the leaves, called chlorosis, with the veins at first remaining green. A shot-in-the-arm treatment may be given by applying one or two pounds of powdered copperas (iron sulphate) to each hundred square feet of bed, and wetting down; even quicker results may be had by spraying with a solution of an ounce of copperas to a gallon of water as suggested for azaleas. These treatments are only temporary, and if there is definite evidence of chlorosis, aluminum sulphate, iron chelates or sulphur should be applied to the soil in addition to the copperas treatment.

Planting. If at all possible, prepare the bed several weeks before the planting is made so that the plant food may become neutralized before the roots of the plants come in contact with it. When it is not practical to prepare the bed in advance as suggested, it would be safer to leave the plant food out and scatter it on top of the bed after the planting is completed. When the bed is finished it should be approximately level with the surrounding surface, so that when it has settled it will be about an inch lower, to facilitate watering and mulching, unless, of course, it is considered necessary to raise the bed to secure proper drainage.

When the plants are received from the nursery they should be unpacked and planted at once, if practicable. If they cannot be planted immediately, the packing should be examined; if found moist, the package may be left intact for twenty-four hours. But if the plants seem to be badly dried out, they may be plunged in water—roots, tops and all—overnight but not longer; then either heel in or plant. This overnight soaking will many times restore plants that are apparently dead.

Most nurseries prune their plants before shipping, but rarely severely enough. As a guide it is suggested that, before planting, tea roses be pruned to six or eight inches and hybrid teas to eight to ten inches. Plantings made late in the spring should be more severely pruned than those made earlier.

Roses should be planted at such a depth that the joint where the budding was done will be barely under the surface. There is as much danger in planting too deep as in not planting deep enough.

If the planting is made very late in the season (at which time the weather will probably be warm), after watering thoroughly, pull a mound of earth up, completely covering each plant, to prevent drying out. This mound must be pulled away gradually after a few weeks.

Cultivation. The everblooming roses must be given such cultural attention as will keep them growing throughout the season if you are to have continuous bloom. During the dry periods

water them copiously at least once every week, heavily enough that the water will reach the deepest roots. Unless the plants are mulched, a light cultivation should be given after each watering; also after each rain. Never cultivate more than an inch or so; deep digging will injure the roots.

Of course, much depends upon the fertility of the soil, but generally speaking it can be assumed that established roses in average soil will need annual applications of commercial **fertilizer** totaling about four pounds per hundred square feet of bed area.

All the plant food should not be given at one time but should be divided into about four equal applications. Any of the dependable garden fertilizers may be used. A very popular one throughout the South analyzes 6–8–8. There are now being used some newer special rose fertilizers that analyze 10–5–5. When they are used, only about half as much should be applied as of the 6–8–8. So far as I know, all are good.

The first application may be made in February, when the plants are pruned and the beds cleaned, and later ones at six-week intervals. Many growers prefer deferring the last feeding of the year until mid-autumn. Discontinue feeding early enough to permit the plants to harden up before winter cold arrives. Much will depend on the season, but in the Upper South this would mean that the last application should be made in early September; in the Middle South, about the middle of the month; and in the Deep South, about the first of October.

Mulches for roses are definitely recommended. Many of the most successful growers are now leaning strongly toward their use. Two to four inches of leaves, straw, pine needles, hay or commercial humus placed on the beds in early summer will eliminate all cultivation, keep the soil cooler and reduce watering to a minimum.

Pruning. Pruning of established plants is one of the most important operations in growing roses. It is impossible to set definite rules as to the time when the pruning should be done or the extent of the cutting. It can be said with safety, however, that the major pruning of bush roses should be done in late winter. The last half of February is usually the best period for the Middle South. By that time you should be able to differentiate clearly between the sound and unsound wood and can remove any that has been winterkilled.

Numerous tests made in private gardens and at experiment stations during the past few years show quite clearly that many of us have been pruning our roses too severely. The many leaves are little factories where food for the plants is manufactured; if we take off too much wood in pruning, or in cutting flowers for the house, we reduce these little food factories to the point where they are not able to meet the demands of the plant. The result is a weak plant, susceptible to attacks by both insects and disease.

As a guide it is suggested that strong-growing varieties such as Peace be pruned back to four or five canes, twelve to fifteen inches long; medium-growing varieties to three to five canes, fifteen to twenty inches long. For the weak varieties, which include many of the yellows and multicolors, about the only pruning necessary is to remove dead and diseased wood and clip a few inches from the longest canes.

One of the Southern experiment station tests indicates that a certain variety pruned to four inches produced an average of 46 blooms to a plant; pruned to twelve inches, 81 blooms to a plant; pruned to twenty inches, 95 blooms to a plant; and, left unpruned, 164 blooms to a plant.

Floribundas will need little pruning except the removal of faded flower heads, but these should be removed regularly, taking off a liberal amount of wood with them.

Insects and Diseases.   Aphids, beetles and thrips are common enemies of those who grow roses. **Aphids** usually attack the new, tender growths, sucking out the juices; **beetles** of different kinds eat leaves and flower buds. An occasional spraying or dusting will usually keep these two groups of insects in check.

Thrips are a bit more troublesome. They are tiny insects which get into the base of the opening flowers and suck juices from the petals, causing the flowers to brown, ball and fail to open properly. Spraying or dusting the tops of the plants regularly during the growing season, and gathering and burning all flowers thought to be infested, should keep these little marauders under control.

The most common as well as the most dangerous rose disease with which the Southern gardener has to deal is **black spot**, a fungus trouble evidenced by small black spots with yellow margins which appear on the leaves, causing them finally to drop off. This trouble does not kill the plants outright but devitalizes them to the point that growth and bloom stop; then, when winter comes, the plants usually succumb to dieback or other disease. Unless we keep black spot under control by the use of a good fungicide which may be found at the seed stores, dieback may be expected.

Black spot is usually more in evidence in spring and early summer, because it rains more frequently at this time. Beginning with early spring and extending to early summer, applications of fungicides should be made at ten-day intervals, with fewer applications during summer, fall and early winter.

Mildew, another fungus disease, is especially bad on many of the ramblers and polyanthas. There are special preparations for the control of mildew available at the seed stores.

23

Lawns

There is no part of the home landscape more important than the lawn. A modest cottage surrounded by a luxuriant, well-kept lawn is appealing, but even a magnificent mansion surrounded by barren soil is lacking in interest. The smallest landscape planting without its proper proportions of lawn is incomplete; in larger plantings the lawn forms an integral part for which there can be no substitute. In all landscape plans and plantings, regardless of their size or location, the grass area is of major importance. It seems inconsistent that a homeowner would spend a considerable sum for the house, trees, shrubs and flowers and then completely fail to include a lawn in his budget.

In nearly every community in the South there are old lawns badly in need of remaking. In many cases, clovers or other legumes will help restore the fertility of the soil and prevent the complete disappearance of the lawn grass. In other cases, the grass has probably been disappearing gradually, over a long period, and little of it is left

PLANTING A NEW LAWN

In view of the average homeowner's reluctance to remake a lawn—and the heavy expenditure in funds and labor that is usually necessary to rejuvenate an old one—it is very important for the work to be done properly in the first place. If the area to be planted has been filled in with poor clay or other soil of uncertain character, as so many of our town and city lots have, or if the lot has been graded down to a point where nothing except poor clay remains, it is necessary to cover the area with several inches of good topsoil before attempting the planting of sod.

In preparing a new lawn in soil of ordinary fertility, spade it to a depth of six or eight inches, or plow or rototill it to that depth if the area is large. After this, mix in lawn food, anywhere from twenty to forty pounds per thousand square feet of area, depending on the character and fertility of the soil and the nitrogen content of the fertilizer.

Rake the area to a level with a fine-toothed rake, and remove stones, clods and foreign matter (such as tree roots, broken brick and concrete) that might interfere with mowing after the lawn has been finished.

Take care to see that all depressions are filled. It is better for the sodded area to have enough slope to facilitate proper drainage.

SOIL ACIDITY

Several years ago the question of acidity of soil for lawns was a controversial one. I ran a test for a few years on about two acres, marking off the area in strips 25 feet in width and liming alternate strips. I could discern no noticeable difference in the growth or color of the grass on the limed and unlimed strips. I will admit, however, that some soils do need an application of lime for adequate growth. In some areas liming is essential. I think the safe thing to do is to take some samples of your soil to your agricultural agent at your county courthouse and be guided by his instructions. He will usually have it analyzed without charge.

Time to Plant. The proper time for planting, especially if sprigging or cuttings are used, depends somewhat upon the season and type of grass used. If this work is done at the beginning of the rainy season, the plants will begin making growth immediately and complete coverage will soon result. In the Middle South, spring is considered the best season for planting. In the Lower South, the beginning of the summer rainy season is probably best.

In the Upper South, where bluegrass is used, early fall is the natural and most favorable time to sow the seeds. Spring seeding often fails, owing to competition of weed seeds, high temperatures and periods of drought which occur before the seedling plants are deeply and firmly rooted. Seeds sown in the fall become established before winter, and in the early spring they start to grow before the weeds appear.

Manner of Planting. If you are planting only a small area, you can get quickest results by sodding solid. This is always the best method on terraces, slopes and other areas where there is the danger of erosion if complete coverage is not obtained in a short time.

For a large area, you may either sod solid, use cuttings, stolons or small cubes of sod, or plant the area to seed if available. Seeding for a permanent lawn, however, is not the general practice in the South, because a good sod is much more quickly obtained by other methods. Seeding, of course, is usually the least expensive of the different methods and can be used very satisfactorily on large areas where there is little danger of serious erosion before good growth develops.

TYPES OF LAWN GRASSES

Bermuda grass (*Cynodon dactylon*). Though a native of the "old country," this grass grows in practically all warm areas throughout the world. It has proved acceptable to a number of soil types, and for most sunny situations it is a desirable lawn grass. However, it is not a satisfactory grass for shady locations, and it is easily crowded out by other grasses, especially Dallis.

The common method of planting Bermuda grass is either to sod solid or to plant cuttings, although the old common Bermuda was seeded. If you use cuttings, make shallow furrows twelve to fifteen inches apart and drop the cuttings along these furrows; then rake the soil back into the furrows, level the area off and water thoroughly.

This grass grows by both underground and surface runners, and if given a good soil and a moderate amount of moisture it will develop a good lawn within weeks after planting. It is hard to keep out of flower beds and borders. The experiment station at Tifton, Georgia, has developed new types of Bermuda, Tiftgreen and Tiftlawn, suitable for golf greens and lawns that are said to stand a fair amount of shade and more abuse than the old forms.

Carpet grass. An excellent grass for semishady locations, carpet grass will thrive under trees if the light is good. It makes fine sod, if given plenty of food and moisture, and is easily kept under control.

Kentucky bluegrass (Poa pratensis). This grass is very popular as a lawn and golf-course grass in many sections of the Upper South, but it tends to die out in the Central and Lower South. It is evergreen, has small leaves of a dark green color and is very desirable in sections where soil and climatic conditions are favorable. It grows especially well in light shade and thrives in alkaline soil with a heavy phosphate content.

Centipede grass. (Eremochloa opliuroides). Centipede grass, like Bermuda, seems to prefer full sunlight for its best growth, but it will stand considerably more shade than Bermuda. It made a better showing under adverse conditions of poor soil and little moisture than any other grass tested, and it is well adapted to porous, light soils. I predict a much wider use of this grass as seeds are now available. I like centipede very much. The color is good, and it requires little mowing. The Florida Experiment Station reports:

Centipede grass has short leaves. It seldom grows more than 3 or 4 inches high. It spreads by means of surface runners and forms a very dense sod. The leaves are intermediate in fineness between

Bermuda and St. Augustine, being somewhat narrower and shorter
than carpet. The seed spikes resemble somewhat those of St.
Augustine, and grow 3 to 4 inches high.

Centipede is more nearly adapted to dry sandy soil than any of
the other grasses. While it becomes wilted and dry under droughty
conditions, it recuperates quickly, and on high dry Norfolk sand it
has crowded out all other grasses.

Centipede grass makes a very attractive lawn with less attention
than any of the other lawn grasses. It requires less water and
mowing and, once established, holds a stand indefinitely. There are
many beautiful lawns of centipede grass growing on high dry sand
as well as on heavier soils, scattered throughout the state.

On our grounds centipede has crowded out and completely
eliminated Bermuda, carpet and St. Augustine when grown adjacent to them. It has proved immune to chinch bugs. Some of
my neighbors report that they have found chinch bugs in their
centipede, but I have two acres of lawn and have found no
chinch bugs during the thirty years we have grown this grass.

St. Augustine grass (*Stenotaphrum secundatum*). A native
of the South, this grass has become very popular in Florida and
along the Gulf Coast as a lawn grass during the last decade. This
grass is not considered hardy, but it went through zero temperatures on my grounds with very little damage. It does not brown
as early in the season as zoysia, Bermuda grass and carpet grass,
and there are luxuriant green lawns of it in central Florida and
farther south, in midwinter.

St. Augustine grass is the most common lawn grass in Florida
and along the Gulf Coast. It is a coarse but tender grass, rank-
growing and vigorous when well fertilized and watered. If the
grass is not mowed, the leaves often attain almost a foot in
length and one-half inch across. It spreads by surface runner and
forms a dense turf under optimum conditions.

St. Augustine grass grows equally well in shade and sunlight
but must at all times have plenty of moisture and plant food in
order to be attractive. It is more resistant to cold than any of
the other lawn grasses generally grown in the South, often re-

maining green throughout the winter. It is adapted to practically all soil types, provided plenty of moisture is present. But St. Augustine lawns mean an eternal fight with chinch bugs.

So far as I know, seeds of St. Augustine grass are not yet available, and it is necessary to propagate from sod or cuttings. If the soil is properly prepared, runners can be taken and cut into six-inch lengths. With a stick or rod about the size of a marking pencil, make a hole in the soil at a very acute angle, about four inches deep. Stick the cutting into the hole and firm down with your foot. This leaves about two inches of the cutting above soil. If the soil is dry, water the cuttings thoroughly. If conditions of moisture are satisfactory, every cutting should take root and begin growth immediately.

Zoysia matrella, sometimes called Manila grass. Although a little slow to become established, this is considered one of the best lawn grasses for the South, particularly if the lawn is well cared for. It has an especially fine leaf, dark green in color. When well grown it produces a very dense sod. It is one of the earliest of the perennial grasses to begin growth in the spring, but in the fall it turns brown with the first heavy frost. Since it attains a height of only three to four inches, it requires little mowing. It is recommended for shade.

Seeds are not available, and plantings are usually made by sodding solid or using two-inch squares of sod, spaced twelve inches apart each way. It usually takes two years to establish a good lawn under this system of planting. Enrich and prepare the soil well for this grass before you plant it. After planting, see that the grass gets plenty of water until it is well established. There are several other forms of zoysia available (Z. *japonica* and Meyers), but those have not proved as popular as *matrella.*

RENEWING AN OLD LAWN

An old lawn that has been neglected for many years may be hard to bring into luxuriant growth and full beauty unless you completely remake it. This is particularly true if the area has been overrun by some obnoxious grass or is badly packed. In this operation, you should completely remove the sod, spade or plow the area, fertilize, and handle it as if you were making an entirely new lawn.

However, many lawns where the grass is thin and the soil loose but lacking in fertility can be restored by top dressing. A quarter to a half inch of good rich topsoil applied twice each season, once in the fall and again in the spring, will restore the average lawn within a few years.

LAWN MAINTENANCE

Nearly everyone who grows shrubbery or flowers realizes that these plants must have cultivation, plant food and water to bring satisfactory results. Yet the same people seem to expect their lawns to go on from year to year giving dense, luxuriant sod without any attention whatsoever except an occasional mowing.

One of the best ways to prevent obnoxious weeds is to smother them by keeping the grass well fed, luxuriant and vigorous. According to my experience, several feedings of the lawn are necessary each year for best growth. Most of the grasses do not give a good rich color unless they are well fed. If you plant winter grass, make one application of plant food then and at least two other applications, one in early spring and another in midsummer.

Use any good lawn fertilizer, about three pounds to a hundred square feet (smaller quantities, of course, will be proportionately helpful). Southern lawn grasses seem to thrive on food with a high nitrogen content. Consult your seed store on what is used in your area.

After each feeding, wet down the sod in order to remove all fertilizer from the grass blades and carry it down to the roots of the grass, where it can be used.

Apply water during the dry season of the year. Let the sprinkler run quite a while before you move it, and make sure the soil is wet to the depth of several inches at each watering. Merely sprinkling the leaves of the grass is injurious.

Begin mowing new lawns when the grass is about two to three inches high. Normally you should continue at weekly intervals during the growing season. Frequent mowings, particularly if the grass is thin, encourage spreading and facilitate quick coverage. During dry periods don't mow as often or as closely as you do when the grass is making normal growth.

It is difficult sometimes to say just how close the grass should be cut. The climate, fertility of soil, moisture and type of grass involved must be given consideration. While a closely clipped lawn gives a neat appearance and permits the sunlight to reach the earth and warm the soil earlier in spring, it can be too closely clipped. One and one half to two inches would be about right. Grass, like most other forms of plant life, needs a certain quantity of leafage in order to be able to manufacture a proper food supply, and persistent close cutting can be injurious.

In order to reduce the possibilities of building up too much thatch, gardeners are urged to use a grass-catcher attachment on their lawn mowers.

WINTER LAWNS

Few developments in recent years have done so much to improve the appearance of Southern home landscapes in winter as the planting of winter lawns. Italian rye grass (*Lolium multiflorum*) is the species usually used in this type of planting. In the Central South and farther north where most of the perennial grasses turn a rusty brown with the coming of frost, rye grass can be depended on to give a brilliant green lawn throughout the winter.

Planting usually occurs during the months of September and October but can be done later. In regions subject to hard freezes, the grass should be sown early enough to become well established before winter; otherwise satisfactory growth may not be made until early spring. It is customary to cut the old sod very close and sow the rye-grass seed at the rate of about five or more pounds to a thousand square feet of area.

For years it was customary in planting rye grass to give a light

covering of sand or topsoil after the seeds were sown. This practice is not now recommended because of the danger of building
up thatch. If the old sod is cut very closely before planting the
seed and given a good watering immediately afterward, most of
the seeds will be washed down to the soil. Unless there is ample
rain, water the lawn frequently, about three times a week for
the first few weeks after planting, to facilitate germination of the
seeds and to encourage the seedlings to become happily anchored
in the soil. If you permit the lawn to dry out while the seeds
are germinating or during the first few weeks thereafter, many
of them will be lost. But if you apply plenty of water, you
should have a brilliant green carpet within a few weeks' time.

Rye grass likes liberal quantities of food. Any good lawn fertilizer, used at the rate of about twenty-five pounds to a thousand
square feet of area, will suffice.

Recent experiments indicate that rye grass is adapted for use
as far north as Oklahoma and the southern part of the Texas
Great Plains. This grass will normally die out with the coming
of summer weather, but as it dies the perennial grass develops
and serves to complete the cycle for a year-round lawn.

Some homeowners in the South claim that the consistent use
of rye grass on winter lawns will result in injury to the permanent sod, but if the lawn is cut close in the spring so that the
sun can reach and warm the soil, it is not thought that injury
will result.

Owing to the thickness of the sod on the average Zoysia lawn,
it is difficult to get the rye-grass seeds down to the soil. For that
reason, many gardeners are reluctant to overplant Zoysia with
rye grass.

24

Ornamental Shrubs

As a group, the ornamental shrubs are very tolerant. Most of them will grow in full sun, practically all will thrive in half shade, and a considerable number will grow and flower abundantly in full shade if the light is good.

Unless we are collecting plants rather than beautifying our grounds, a garden is not built merely to contain shrubs and flowers. We design our planting and then use shrubs and flowers just as an artist uses paints: to build up a picture. With this purpose in mind we should decide precisely what we wish to achieve with our plant material and buy each plant with a specific function in mind.

The importance of selecting shrubs with a view to obtaining continuous bloom over as long a period as possible cannot be overlooked. By careful selection, we can, in the Central South, have bloom in the shrubbery borders and beds every month in the year. Of course, we cannot expect in January the same abundance of color that greets us in the spring, but there may be sufficient winter bloom to give us a touch of color and to hold our interest.

WHEN TO PLANT

You may begin in the late fall when the leaves are falling from the deciduous trees. Early planting enables the plants to become established and new roots to be formed by the time spring arrives. Shrubs planted early usually give much better growth the first year and require much less watering. Container-grown shrubs and roses may be planted any time if carefully handled.

When planting in beds and borders, the entire area should be spaded and enriched, and, if practicable, this work should be done at least a few weeks before the actual planting is done. An application of plant food or about three pounds of commercial fertilizer (6–8–8) to each hundred square feet of bed should be scattered over the area and spaded in.

HOW TO PLANT

When the shrubs arrive from a distance, unpack them as soon as practicable. Conifers and large broad-leaved evergreens are usually shipped "B & B" (balled and burlapped) and, when so received, should be handled by the ball, not by the trunk, in order to prevent breaking loose the soil around the roots and thus injuring the root system.

Deciduous shrubs are usually received with bare roots and may sometimes appear to be dried out. If so, they should be submerged in water, tops and all, overnight, but no longer. In any event, soaking the roots of bare-root shrubs for a few hours before planting will generally prove highly beneficial; this, of course, is not necessary if they are out of the ground for only a few hours.

Soil. Any ordinary soil will satisfy the great majority of our garden shrubs. Azaleas, andromedas, camellias, leucothoës, and rhododendrons require a soil well filled with humus and strongly acid; a soil with a pH of 4.5 to 5.5 will satisfy most of this group. Most other broad-leaved evergreens prefer a soil that is at least slightly acid.

The hole for each plant should be several inches deeper and broader than actually necessary to accommodate the root system, so that several inches of topsoil, with which a liberal quantity of leaf mold, peat moss or sawdust has been mixed, can be placed in the bottom of the hole before the plant is set. As a

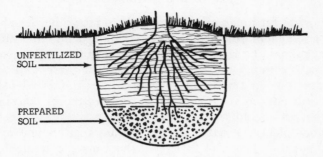

UNFERTILIZED SOIL →

PREPARED SOIL →

In planting bare-root roses and shrubs, be generous in digging the hole. Make it large enough to let the roots spread out naturally.

rule, it is not necessary to remove the burlap from balled plants, as it will soon decay. If the plant is small and the material exceptionally strong, it may be slit in several places with a sharp knife.

In the case of bare-root plants, several inches of the soil mixture should go into the hole before the plant is placed, and the same kind of soil used for filling in about the roots, which should be spread out naturally without any cramping; it is better to prune the roots than to bend and crowd them into the hole. After filling the hole two thirds full of soil, fill with water to settle the soil about the roots; when this has soaked in, finish filling with soil and pack down.

As a rule, shrubs may be set an inch deeper than they grew in the nursery; when the planting is completed, there should be a slight depression around each plant to hold mulches and moisture and to facilitate watering.

Spacing. Most persons are all too desirous of getting quick results from their shrubbery plantings and place fast-growing, large-type shrubs and small trees where smaller-sized material would be more desirable. Trees most assuredly have their place in the landscape plan, but they should not be used where shrubs are appropriate. We should always give consideration to the ultimate size and height of the pieces, picturing the planting as it will look not next year but five years from today.

This desire for quick effect also leads to crowding the plants. While no definite rule can be given for spacing the various species, it should be kept in mind that most of the landscape-size shrubs will, within a few years, be twice their present size, and room must be left for this development. For the dwarf plants, three feet is not too much, and the majority of the garden shrubs should have five feet or more.

Crowded plants not only look less pleasing than those properly spaced, but the blanket of foliage excludes air and sunlight and subjects the shrubs to injury from insects and disease. When very small shrubs are used, there could be no objection to spacing them half the usual distance, with a view to taking out alternate plants after two or three years.

If the planting is large enough to justify it, a much better effect may be obtained by planting three or more shrubs of one kind in a group. Such plantings give the effect of mass, so valuable in creating a pleasing landscape composition.

PRUNING

Pruning is one of the most important of all garden operations, and it is rather disconcerting to see, almost everywhere we go, the extent to which lovely shrubbery plantings are being indiscriminately butchered under a pretext of pruning.

By the proper use of the pruning knife sickly shrubs may be restored to life, bloom may be materially increased and foliage developed, the shape of the plant may be changed and its character of growth improved and many of the large-growing species may be kept down for years.

But let us always be sure we have a definite purpose in mind before a single branch is cut. Unless pruning is for a definite purpose, it is far better left undone. May I suggest in all earnestness that to turn this important work over to unknown persons who call at the door is inviting disaster. Either personally supervise the pruning or turn it over to someone of known competence.

As a rule, shrubs need little or no pruning the first year after planting, but thereafter most of them benefit by having some of the oldest wood removed near the ground. If this is done each year, the shrubs can be kept in a healthy, growing condition without the loss of any great amount of wood at one time. If, however, the pruning is neglected for several years, it may become necessary to remove so much wood that the beauty of the plant will be destroyed for a season.

"Topping" not only spoils the appearance of shrubs but induces the development of a thick top growth which sunlight is unable to penetrate and which makes a haven for insects and diseases. If the plant is to be pruned, take out some of the old wood as near the ground as practicable, but never top it.

If the shrub has been neglected for several years, it may be necessary to cut it off entirely, near the ground, and permit it to renew itself; but in most cases we may be able to restore such plants by removing approximately one third of the wood each year for three years, thus obtaining an entirely new plant in that period without greatly diminishing the beauty of the subject.

Most shrubs are far more pleasing when permitted to develop naturally, and shearing should be confined strictly to the formal garden. The acme of success in pruning is to leave the plant so that it does not appear to have been pruned at all.

Generally speaking, shrubs which flower in early spring form their flower buds on old wood and should be pruned in spring just after the flowers have faded. If these shrubs are pruned in winter, the flower buds will be removed and there will be few, if any, flowers in the spring. Vitex, althea, Anthony Waterer spirea, roses and others which flower on new wood during the summer should have their heaviest pruning in winter. A light pruning, cultivating, watering and feeding will usually serve to lengthen considerably the flowering season of the summer-flowering shrubs.

FEEDING

Shrubs of all kinds require food and should be given at least one good feeding each year. Commercial food should be applied in very late winter or early spring, at the rate of about three pounds to each hundred square feet of bed, and raked in.

Most of the shrubbery plantings in the South suffer from drought, and for this reason they should have a heavy mulch of straw, leaves or commercial humus, which will go a long way in conserving moisture, lessening the necessity for cultivation and adding to the fertility of the soil.

SPRING-FLOWERING SHRUBS TO BE PRUNED
AFTER BLOOM HAS FADED

Azaleas in variety
Barberry
Deutzia
Dogwood (Cornus)
Elder (Sambucus)
Forsythia
Fringe tree
   (Chionanthus)
Hydrangea hortensis
Japanese quince
   (*Chaenomeles
   japonica*)

Mock orange
   (Philadelphus)
Pearlbush
   (Exochorda)
Redbud (Cercis)
Rhododendrons in
   variety
Snowball
   (*Viburnum
   opulus sterile*)
Spireas, early
   flowering

Sweet shrub
   (*Calycanthus
   floridus*)
Weigela
Winter honeysuckle
   (*Lonicera
   fragrantissima*)

SUMMER-FLOWERING SHRUBS
TO BE PRUNED IN WINTER

Althea
   (*Hibiscus
   syriacus*)
Bush clover
   (Desmodium)
Butterfly bush
   (Buddleia)
Chaste tree
   (Vitex)

Crape myrtle
   (Lagerstroemia)
High-bush
   cranberry
   (*Viburnum
   opulus*)
*Hydrangea
   paniculata*
Roses, common
   everblooming

Smoke tree
   (*Rhus cotinus*)
Spirea
   Anthony Waterer
   S. *billiardi*
   S. *douglasi*
Sweet pepperbush
   (*Clethra
   alnifolia*)

DWARF SHRUBS FOR BORDERS AND
IN FRONT OF TALLER SPECIES

Azalea, Japanese
Deutzia gracilis
Dwarf cape jasmine
(*Gardenia
radicans*)
*Hypericum
moserianum*

Junipers, dwarf
Lavender
(Lavandula)
Ligustrum
L. coriaceum
L. ioandrum

Serissa foetida
Spirea, Anthony
Waterer
Symphoricarpos
(both coralberry
and snowberry)

TALL SHRUBS AND EVERGREENS
FOR BACKGROUNDS

Althea (*Hibiscus
syriacus*)
Camellias in variety
Crape myrtle
(Lagerstroemia)
Deutzia
Dogwood (Cornus)
Fringe tree
(Chionanthus)
Holly (Ilex)
I. cornuta
I. decidua
I. opaca
I. vomitoria

Juniper
English
Irish
Ketlers
Laland firethorn
(*Pyracantha
coccinea lalandi*)
Ligustrum
L. japonicum
L. lucidum
Mock orange
(*Philadelphus
coronarius*)
Pearlbush
(Exochorda)

Redbud (Cercis)
Smoke tree
(*Rhus cotinus*)
Sweet shrub
(*Calycanthus
floridus*)
Tamarix
Tatarian
honeysuckle
(*Lonicera
tatarica*)
Viburnum
V. carlesi
V. opulus
Weigela rosea

SHRUBS GROWN FOR THEIR FRUITS

Aralia
Ardisia
Barberry
Coralberry
(*Symphoricarpos
vulgaris*)

Cotoneasters in
variety
Dogwood (Cornus)
Elaeagnus
Elder (Sambucus)
Euonymus

Firethorn
(Pyracantha)
French mulberry
(*Callicarpa
americana*)

SHRUBS GROWN FOR THEIR FRUITS (cont.)

Hawthorn
(Crataegus)
Heavenly bamboo
(*Nandina
domestica*)
High-bush
cranberry
(*Viburnum
opulus*)

Holly (Ilex) in
variety, esp.
I. decidua
I. opaca
Ligustrums in
variety

Snowberry
(*Symphoricarpos
racemosus*)
Tatarian
honeysuckle
(*Lonicera
tatarica*)

SHRUBS WITH HIGHLY COLORED FOLIAGE

Arborvitae (Thuja),
golden and
variegated
Golden elder
(*Sambucus
aurea*)

Japanese maple
(*Acer palmatum*)
Ligustrum, golden
and variegated
Photinia glabra

Purple-leaf barberry
(*Berberis
thunbergii
purpurea*)
Weigela variegata

SHRUBS FOR SHADY PLACES

Andromeda (Pieris)
Arrowwood
(*Viburnum
dentatum*)
Azaleas in variety
Box
Camellia
  C. japonica
  C. sasanqua
Dogwood (Cornus)

Fringe tree
(Chionanthus)
Japanese maple
(*Acer palmatum*)
Leucothoë racemosa
Mountain laurel
(*Kalmia latifolia*)
Redbud (Cercis)
Rhododendrons in
variety

Silverbell (Halesia)
Sweet shrub
(*Calycanthus
floridus*)
Wax myrtle
(Myrica)
Witch hazel
(Hamamelis)

*All the broad-leaved evergreens will thrive in partial shade; many of
them in full shade.*

SHRUBS FOR MOIST SITUATIONS

Andromeda (Pieris)
Buttonbush
  (*Cephalanthus
  occidentalis*)
Chokeberry
  (Aronia)
Elder
  (Sambucus)
Ilex glabra
Leucothoë racemosa

Red-osier dogwood
  (*Cornus
  stolonifera*)
Spiraea tomentosa
Swamp azalea
  (*Azalea viscosa*)
Swamp rose
  (*Rosa palustris*)

Sweet pepperbush
  (*Clethra
  alnifolia*)
Sweet shrub
  (*Calycanthus
  floridus*)

SHRUBS FOR LATE WINTER BLOOM

Azalea
Camellia
Corylopsis

Japanese quince
  (*Chaenomeles
  japonica*)
Primrose jasmine
  (*Jasminum
  primulinum*)

Winter honeysuckle
  (*Lonicera
  fragrantissima*)
Winter jasmine
  (*Jasminum
  nudiflorum*)

SHRUBS FOR SPRING BLOOM

Azalea
Camellia
Crab apple (Malus)
Deutzia
Dogwood (Cornus)
Hawthorn
  (Crataegus)
Japanese magnolia

Japanese quince
  (*Chaenomeles
  japonica*)
Kerria
Loropetalum
Mock orange
  (Philadelphus)
Pearlbush
  (Exochorda)

Redbud (Cercis)
Spirea
  S. prunifolia
  S. reevesiana
  S. thunbergii
  S. vanhouttei
Viburnum
  V. carlesi
  V. opulus

SHRUBS FOR SUMMER BLOOM

Abelia grandiflora
Althea (*Hibiscus
  syriacus*)
Butterfly bush
  (Buddleia)
Buttonbush
  (*Cephalanthus
  occidentalis*)
*Ceanothus
  americanus*
Chaste tree (Vitex)
Crape myrtle
  (Lagerstroemia)

Dwarf pomegranate
  (*Punica granatum
  rubra*)
Elder (Sambucus)
Flowering senna
  (Cassia)
Gardenia
Hydrangea
  H. hortensis
  *H. paniculata
   grandiflora*
  H. quercifolia

Lantana
Mock orange
  (*Philadelphus
  virginalis*)
Oleander (Nerium)
Spirea
  Anthony Waterer
  S. billiardi
Swamp rose (*Rosa
  palustris*)
*Viburnum
  suspensum*

SHRUBS FOR LATE SUMMER AND FALL BLOOM

Althea (*Hibiscus
  syriacus*)
Butterfly bush
  (Buddleia)
Chaste tree (Vitex)

Flowering senna
  (Cassia)
Gardenia
Lantana

Spirea
  Anthony Waterer
  S. billiardi
  S. tomentosa
Sweet pepperbush
  (*Clethra
  alnifolia*)

SHRUBS FOR FALL AND EARLY WINTER BLOOM

Ardisia
Camellia sasanqua
Duranta
Elaeagnus

Lantana
Sweet olive
  (*Osmanthus
  fragrans*)

Tea plant (*Thea
  sinensis*)
Witch hazel
  (Hamamelis)

25

Propagation of Ornamentals

Ornamental plants may be propagated in a variety of ways, including seeds, layering, cuttings and several forms of grafting.

The annual flowers which form a very important sector of practically every Southern garden are grown from seeds, and they usually "come true." (See Chapter 13.) Many biennials and perennials are also grown from seeds, but the perennials do not always come true. They have not become "fixed" to the point where we can always depend on the seedling being identical with the mother variety. Some of the annuals also have a tendency to revert to inferior types unless the seed plants are selected very carefully. Seeds to be planted should come only from plants that show proper color and flower formation.

Since many perennials do not come true from seed, they are usually propagated by divisions or cuttings from the mother plant.

Many kinds of evergreens, flowering shrubs and roses, as well as some ornamental trees, may easily be propagated by the home gardener. This home propagation does not involve any expensive tools or equipment.

CUTTINGS

Propagation by cuttings is perhaps the method most commonly used by the home gardener, since this method ensures that the new plants will have characteristics similar to their parents. There are two seasons for taking cuttings in the South. Along the Gulf Coast and in the Lower South, one may begin taking summer cuttings about the last of May and continue until midsummer or later. In the Middle and Upper South, the material is usually not sufficiently mature to begin taking cuttings until about the first of June, but one may continue until late summer. In my area, cuttings of azaleas taken in early June and handled properly can be expected to form good roots in four weeks. Cuttings from roses, spring-flowering shrubs and most evergreens root best when they are taken in early summer, but it is necessary to keep summer cuttings covered securely to prevent escape of moisture and humidity.

Summer cuttings seem to root better in a half-and-half mixture of peat moss and coarse sand. The cuttings should be made with a slanting cut at the lower end, just below a leaf bud, and may be from three to three and a half inches long. Strip the leaves of the lower half of each cutting, dip the base end first in water and then in a rooting stimulant, and lastly tap the cutting on the side of the jar to remove any excess stimulant. Insert each cutting to about one half its length in the rooting medium. The cuttings may be closely spaced. A six-inch flower pot should hold from ten to fifteen cuttings. After they are placed in the pot, spray lightly with water. Now place the flower pot inside a freezer bag, twist the top of the bag and close with a rubber band or freezer tape. This forms a little greenhouse which is vapor proof, and the cuttings should need no more water until they are well rooted.

If you have a large quantity of cuttings they may be placed in a tightly closed cutting bed, but they should be shaded from the midday sun. If placed in a pot, they should be set in a window where there is good light, but never in direct sunlight.

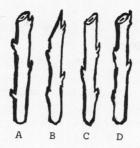

Four cuttings, showing the branch: A, properly cut, just below a leaf bud; B, cut with too long a slope; C, cut too far above the leaf bud; and D, cut too close to the leaf bud.

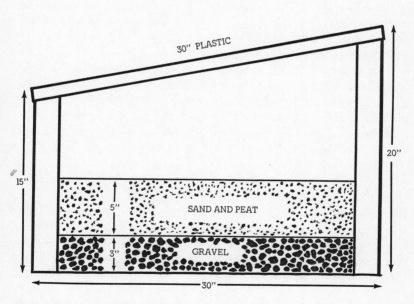

Enough scrap lumber can usually be found around the house to construct a small cutting bed adequate for the use of the home gardener.

Direct sunlight will kill the cuttings regardless of whether they are placed in a cutting bed or a window.

My good Woman Friday has a kind of mania for propagating plants; she uses many methods, and containers of various sizes and shapes. Her current madness is using what I, for the want of a better name, call the "jelly-roll" method. She takes a piece of sheet plastic (maybe it's polyethylene to you) of any small size, let us say eight by twelve inches, and spreads a thin layer of thoroughly damp (but not dripping) sphagnum moss across its greatest width. Then, after dipping the ends of the cuttings in rooting hormone, she lays them on the moss, spaced an inch or less apart. She then folds the edge of the plastic over the ends of the cuttings and, beginning at one side, rolls the whole in a tight roll, secures it with a rubber band, then places it in a window where the light is good. As a rule the cuttings will require no more moisture, but she always examines hers after about two weeks just to make sure. It is certainly a simple, easy way to handle a few cuttings.

Summer cuttings of most plants, if properly cared for, should root in from one to three months. Ordinarily, summer cuttings will need very little attention after they are placed in the pot or cutting bed. However, when using a rooting bed I usually take the cover off the bed and sprinkle the cuttings lightly every week for the first month. If this method is followed, be sure to replace the cover tightly so there will be no leakage of moisture.

Winter cuttings are usually taken in the South in late fall and early winter. November and December are the best months for the Middle South. They may be slightly longer than summer cuttings, say from four to six inches in length, and are usually not covered. Most species of flowering shrubs will root well in the open if taken at the proper season. If garden space is not plentiful, you may root a considerable number of winter cuttings on the north side of a fence or the garage wall. In this case it is suggested that a trench be dug about eight inches wide and eight inches deep and filled with a mixture of equal parts of soil, sand and peat moss. The mixture should be wet down and the cuttings, the lower ends of which should be cut just under

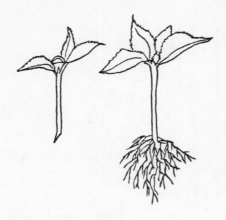

An azalea cutting before and after rooting.

a leaf bud, inserted to about half their length. Most of them will be well rooted by late spring. The ones that are not may be left in the rooting medium until fall. If they are not moved until fall, be sure to keep them well watered during the summer months.

LAYERING

Soil Layering. Branches of many plants when wounded and covered with soil will grow roots at the place of the wound. There are many methods of layering, but perhaps the easiest for the home gardener is wounding and burying a single branch in the soil, leaving only its tip protruding.

Before making a layer, work up the soil where the branch is to be layered, mixing in a quantity of sand and peat moss. The operation involves the wounding of the branch by making a slanting cut from one to two inches long on the lower side of the branch, about ten or fifteen inches from the tip. Dust the cut with a rooting stimulant, then fasten the branch in the soil by using a wooden peg or wire wicket. You may even use a heavy stone, piece of concrete or, if the branch is small, a brick to hold the branch in place. Cover the branch with two or three inches

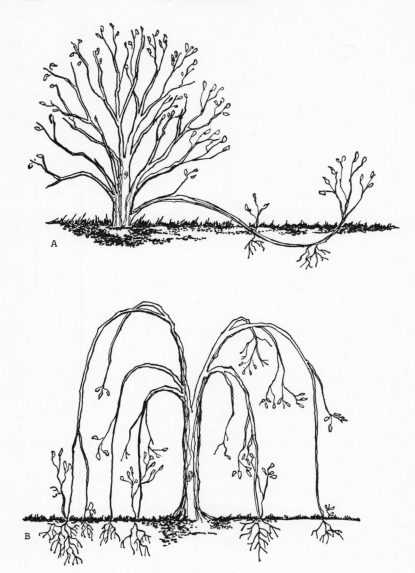

A

B

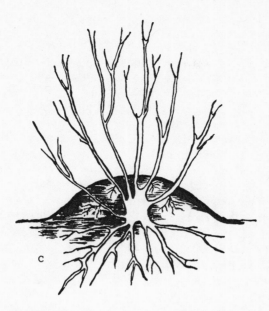

Propagation by layering: A, a ground-layered branch; B, layers made by covering tips of the branches; C, layers made by mounding soil over the crown of the plant.

of the soil and peat moss mixture. Pull the tip of the branch in a semi-erect position and mound with soil to hold it in that position. Keep the layer well watered. In a few weeks, a new set of roots should form. When this happens, remove the layer from the mother plant by severing at the base of the new roots.

Some plants may be rooted by pulling branches several feet long down to the earth and giving them the treatment suggested. Sometimes a plant which has numerous branches from the crown, like the honeysuckles and jasmines, may be layered by mounding about six inches of soil over the crown and leaving it there through one growing season. Many of the canes will have grown new roots and may be severed from the mother plant and treated as new specimens. Late spring and early summer are good periods for making layerings.

Air Layering. At the seed and plant stores, gardeners may now find complete kits that will simplify air layering. The operator will need a sharp knife, plastic electrical tape, plastic sheets, sphagnum moss and rooting stimulant.

Branches one year old seem to give best results for air layering. Older branches may form roots but will require a longer period. Air layerings are usually made about twelve or fifteen inches from the ends of the branches. All leaves are removed from a space of about six inches where the layer is to be made. You will need to wound the branch by removing the bark from an area about an inch long halfway around the branch. Some gardeners make a slit with a sharp knife through the middle of the branch and insert a piece of straw or sliver of wood in the cut to keep it open. Next, you will need a ball of sphagnum moss about the size of a baseball, which has been wet and squeezed to remove excess water; dust the wound with the rooting stimulant, then wrap the damp sphagnum moss around the branch, covering the wound.

With a piece of plastic about eight or ten inches long wrap the wound tightly so that the plastic overlaps itself. Before the job is complete, press the ends of the plastic sheeting around the branch and fasten securely with plastic tape. If you do not have tape available, just tie the ends tightly with a piece of twine.

Air layers should not be disturbed during the first growing season. Branches layered in May or June should normally form a good root system by fall. Roots should be visible through the plastic covering, and when they have formed in sufficient number the branch may be severed just below the roots and treated as a new plant.

It is usually considered unnecessary to apply more water to an air layer, but I have found that where the layers are left in full sun they sometimes dry out before roots are formed, in which case it is necessary to open the layered branch carefully, wet it and retie.

Some shrubs and trees are considered very difficult to propagate by cuttings or layers. Among these we would list andromeda,

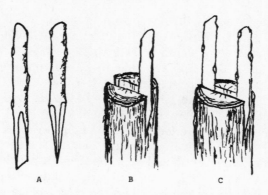

Propagation by grafting: A, scions ready for the graft; B, scion placed in a stock; C, two scions placed in the same stock. If only one is wanted, the weaker may be removed after growth begins.

blue spruce, red cedar, ginkgo, golden rain tree, mountain laurel, locust, mimosa, myrica, pine, fir and hemlock.

GRAFTS

Every gardener, especially in the camellia belt, should know how to make grafts. As most Southern gardeners are willing to divide their flowers with their friends, many of these can be grafted on root stock to produce a new plant of flowering size in about two years.

For grafts to be successful, the scion and root stock must be closely related. For example, you would want to graft a red leaf maple on a stock of the native species, or a pink dogwood on the stock of a native white one.

Cleft grafts are largely used in grafting ornamentals in the South. These grafts should be made in late winter while both scion and stock are dormant. For scions, wood of the previous year's growth is best. Stock of almost any size may be used, but in grafting camellias I prefer stocks from one half to one and one half inches in diameter. The stock for a cleft graft should be cut near the ground with sharp pruning shears, or, if of larger size, a saw may be used. With a chisel, or stout knife, split the end of the stock to a depth of at least two inches and place a wedge or screw driver in the split to hold it open. The scion should be prepared wedge-shaped at the lower end. It is customary for each scion to include three leaf buds, and it should be cut about an inch below the lowest bud.

After the scion is inserted in the split in the stock with the lowest bud to the outside, the wedge may be removed and the pressure from the stock should hold the scion in position.

It is of the utmost importance that the cambium layers—that layer of cells between the bark and the wood—come in contact. If these cambium layers do not come in contact with each other, the grafts will not grow. This would mean that the scion should be placed at the extreme outer edge of the split in the stock. Many gardeners place two scions in each stock and later eliminate the weaker one if both grow.

There are several methods of treating the grafts after they are made. Some gardeners coat all exposed cut surfaces with grafting wax or tree-coating compound. I usually place a handful of wet sphagnum moss around the wound and pull soil up to cover the moss. It once was the practice to cover all cleft grafts with glass jars, but a far simpler method is to pull a plastic bag over the grafts and tie securely around the stock. Be careful not to dislodge the scion.

Cleft grafts can be made on any size stock. Until a severe freeze killed them, I had fifteen varieties of camellias growing on one stock. Normally cleft grafts are placed within a few inches of the ground, but all of these were placed from three to four feet above the ground.

26

Climbing Plants

Is there a section of your grounds that you would like to conceal from view? Would you like to dress up your garage? Is there a fence that could be improved by the tracery of green foliage? Or would the porch be more inviting and more comfortable with a bit of summer sun screened out? Then by all means consider the vines.

ANNUAL VINES

Annual vines grow in a hurry; many of them give fairly good effects within a few weeks after planting. They require little attention, and most of them retain their foliage and bloom until frost cuts them down. They are practically free from disease, and the few insects that attack them can be easily controlled by ordinary spraying or dusting methods.

As a group, **morning glories** are perhaps the most important of these annual climbers. A newcomer to the South is Darling, a giant-flowered type, brilliant rose-cerise in color with a pure white throat. The flowers range up to four inches across. The foliage is a good dark green but not especially heavy. Unlike most morning glories, Darling keeps its blooms open well into the afternoon, and it continues to produce blossoms right up until frost.

Most people who love morning glories never tire of Heavenly Blue and its near relatives, Blue Star and Heavenly Blue Improved. They are vigorous growers and bloom in profusion. Clarke's Early Heavenly Blue comes into bloom a week or ten days before the other strains.

Pearly Gates is an All-America Silver Medal winner of several years ago that lives up to the honor conferred on it. A clear shining white, it is effective alone or in combination with the colors. Scarlett O'Hara, introduced as the first really red morning glory, is an All-America Gold Medal winner of years ago and is still quite popular. Crimson Rambler produces a wealth of ruby red flowers and has the same lush, rich foliage as its blue and white cousins.

Rosie O'Grady is a pleasing rose color which blooms profusely and lasts well into the day. This is a vigorous grower that comes into bloom early in the season. Candy Pink is said to be the first pure pink morning glory, and it is certainly a lovely one. It will bloom from early summer until frost.

Rose Marie is a very lovely little rose-colored morning glory. It is full double, quick growing and free flowering. It will have some single flowers, perhaps, but at least 50 percent come double.

There are a number of other lovely morning glories which you will find listed in the catalogs, the seeds of which are also found at most seed stores.

If you don't need heavy screens or shade, you have a choice of many appealing lighter vines. The old **cypress vine** (*Quamoclit pennata*) is one of the daintiest of all climbers. Its finely cut foliage is lovely, and its small trumpet-shaped flowers are exceptionally dainty. There are two colors, scarlet and white. **Cardinal climber** is very close kin to the cypress vine, but has heavier foliage and larger flowers.

Cathedral bells (*Cobaea scandens*), also called **cup-and-saucer vine,** has a purple, bell-shaped flower and grows rapidly after it once gets started, often attaining a height of twenty to thirty feet. It climbs by means of tendrils and will cling to walls of various kinds.

The **scarlet runner bean** (*Phaseolus coccineus*) is an old climber, but age does not lessen its appeal. The foliage is good, and the red flowers are bright and gay.

Several of the old ornamentals are enjoying a return to popularity. The **balsam apple** (*Momordica balsamina*) which grew on Grandmother's porch is again listed in the catalogs. Its brilliant yellow fruits burst to reveal a bright red inside that is quite spectacular. The **ornamental gourds**, too, are staging a comeback, and for good reason. They are attractive on the vine, make interesting material for indoor decoration and are quite easy to grow.

If you want something just to trail over a porch or window box, black-eyed Susans and trailing nasturtiums are good material. Some of the less vigorous morning glories like Scarlett O'Hara, when pinched back a few times, make ideal trailers; in fact, some of them seem to prefer trailing to climbing.

Late April and early May is a good time to plant annual vines. Give them sunshine, a fairly good soil and a moderate amount of moisture; they will do the rest.

PERENNIAL VINES

Where complete coverage is desired, there are several ivies that should be considered. The evergreen **English ivy** (*Hedera helix*) is one of the best. It makes a dense ground cover and will grow and thrive in the deepest shade. It attaches itself to any kind of wall and to trees by means of minute cups at the ends of the tendrils. This ivy does not penetrate the wood, but it could cause damage to wooden walls owing to the heavy foliage excluding sunlight and air. This is particularly true in areas having heavy rainfall.

If lighter evergreen coverage is needed, there are two or more good **roses** that should be mentioned. Dr. W. Van Fleet is an old yet popular rose, with practically evergreen foliage in the Middle South, and in spring the plants are a mass of lovely light pink blooms. It blooms only once a year, but its surpassing beauty in spring makes it entirely worthwhile. Another good climbing rose, practically evergreen in the Middle South, is the pure single white, Silver Moon. It, like the Van Fleet, blooms only in the spring, but it makes a great display at that season.

Those of us who are familiar with the old French Quarter in New Orleans are always impressed with the extravagant use which has been made of the **climbing fig** (*Ficus pumila*). It has rather small leaves and clings to walls of all heights. The tracery of this vine on light-colored walls presents an unforgettable picture.

There are several native evergreen vines which are perfectly at home on the home grounds. We will first mention **scarlet honeysuckle** (*Lonicera sempervirens*). It has attractive blue-green foliage and produces its trumpet-shaped scarlet flowers during the spring and summer. There is also a yellow form of this honeysuckle available.

Perhaps the native vine which carries the heaviest tradition of the old South is the **yellow jasmine** (*Gelsemium sempervirens*). It is one of the first native vines to bloom in spring and makes a great show with its profusion of yellow flowers. Another native vine, widely used for decorations at Christmas time, for weddings and other festive occasions, is the evergreen **smilax** (*S. lanceolata*), a native of the Gulf Coast states. It is a high-climbing evergreen with large tubers.

For light, airy situations, perhaps one of the best is Queen's wreath (*Antigonon leptopus*), also known as coral vine or Rosa de Montana. It climbs to considerable heights but in the Middle South is usually killed back; however, it comes out from the crown in the spring. It has attractive light green, heart-shaped foliage, and its profusion of rich pink flowers lasts for many weeks. It is considered one of our loveliest climbers.

Silver lace (*Polygonum aubertii*) is a fast-growing, woody, climbing vine with profuse greenish-white fragrant flowers, easy to grow and very desirable.

The hybrid **clematis** varieties are good for situations where heavy foliage is not desired. The flowers of the hybrids are several inches across and make a great display when in bloom. Popular varieties are Duchess of Edinburgh and Henryi, both white; Jackmani, purple; Ramona, lavender; and Mme. Edouard André, red.

In Florida, along the Gulf Coast and in the Rio Grande Valley, where the winters are not too severe, the **alamanda** is popular. The large, lily-shaped yellow flowers attract much attention when the winter temperature will permit it to be grown.

Many perennial climbers have a tendency to produce little growth near the ground, leaving open spaces at the base of the plants which make them undesirable for use as screens. This problem can be corrected to a material degree by training the young vines as laterals along a fence or wire parallel with the surface. The resulting growth will tend to be upright and will give satisfactory coverage from the ground up.

27

Gardening Indoors

Nearly everyone, even here in the South, recognizes
the cheerfulness that a few growing plants add to the interior of
a house, especially during the winter months when outdoor gardening is reduced to a minimum. Indoor gardening has always
been fairly popular throughout the country, but the fashion in
house plants has changed considerably during recent years. In
most homes the old flower stands with their large pots and jar-
dinieres have given way to window gardens and indoor planters
which are more refined and take up much less room. The florists,
seedsmen and ten cent stores have made available a wide variety
of dainty little plants, which, owing to their character of growth,
their small size and unusual refinements, are much better adapted
to use in the modern living unit than the large plants of the
old days.

The indoor garden should be planned with the same care and
attention to detail that is given the outdoor planting. If you are
interested in only a few plants for individual containers, to be
grown for their individual interest and beauty, less planning is
necessary. On the other hand, if you want to develop a window
garden as a feature of your decorating scheme, you should plan
it in detail, particularly the framework.

If you center the planting around a particular window, use

the wide shelf at the base for the larger containers. Work out in detail the plants for this shelf, as well as those for the side framework and central section of the planting, so you will have perfect harmony.

Although our mothers knew little, and probably cared less, about the scientific care of plants and the chemical components of soil, the plants they grew were generally vigorous and healthy. They seemed to know how much food was necessary and were able to discern moisture requirements from experience. The open houses of that day were conducive to the healthy growth of plants. An old lady who lived a few blocks behind my home some years ago grew in tin buckets some of the finest ferns and geraniums I have ever seen. Her ferns were always a vigorous green, and the geraniums bloomed profusely. Her rickety old cabin and open fireplace did not permit overheating.

Many of our modern houses are far too hot and dry for most plants. Plants that have been growing vigorously on the porch during the summer may show signs of illness within a few days after they are moved indoors, especially if the temperature is high and the humidity low. But with a little understanding of the needs of the different species of plants, you will find it not at all difficult to grow plants that will make your home more cheerful and livable. If your house is small, you will not need a large collection of plants—just a few choice ones will do much to make the interior interesting and appealing.

SOIL

As with the outdoor garden, one of the first matters to be considered in growing plants indoors is the soil. While the plants vary in their requirements, you can make a general-purpose soil that will satisfy most of them from 3 parts garden loam, 2 parts peat moss, 1 part sand and 1 part dehydrated cow or sheep manure.

If neither manure is available, use one of the popular garden fertilizers and apply it according to the directions. This general-purpose soil will meet the requirements of most plants grown

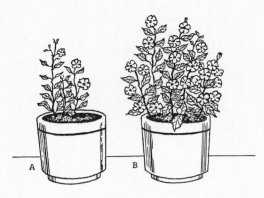

The importance of regular feedings: A, a plant that has not been properly fed; B, one that has had adequate nourishment.

indoors and can be used as a soil base for plants with special requirements. For cacti and succulents, the soil should be highly porous, and one additional part of coarse sand or fine gravel should be added. Old bricks crushed into small pieces are even better. Acid-loving plants, including azaleas, ferns and gardenias, may have an extra part of peat or oak leaf mold added.

FOOD AND WATER

After the plants are growing, give them regular feedings. Just a little food at a time, every four or six weeks, should keep them growing vigorously. Any one of the well-known garden fertilizers can be used. I find the liquid form of plant food very convenient and satisfactory. Most garden fertilizers have the directions on the containers, and they should be closely followed at all times. But regardless of the form of food used, keep it away from the leaves and stems of the plant.

Plants differ, of course, in their moisture requirements. Some of them—geraniums, for example—should be kept on what the florists call the "dry" side, while ferns and begonias prefer liberal quantities of moisture. The atmosphere is so dry in many of our houses during the winter months that plants do not get enough moisture. If the containers are small, the air dry and temperatures high, frequent watering will be necessary. It is better to water thoroughly twice each week than lightly every day. Study the requirements of the individual plants and try to give them what they need.

Pouring a little water on the top of the soil does not always water the plant. Many times only the upper inch or two of soil is wet. This encourages the roots to come to the surface, when they should grow toward the bottom of the pot. Use enough water to wet the soil to the bottom of the container. If you have any doubt, set the container in a pan of water and let it remain until the moisture reaches the surface.

POTTING AND REPOTTING

When selecting pots for plants, use the smallest size that will properly accommodate the mass of roots. Some plants do not bloom well unless they are slightly pot-bound. Place pieces of broken flower pots or small stones in the bottom of the pot in order to ensure drainage. After the soil is firmly set, the surface should be about one quarter of an inch below the edge of the pot. When repotting, extend your fingers on either side of the plant stem, invert the pot and tap the edge lightly against some solid object. The entire contents of the pot will usually come out intact. It is not necessary to repot all plants annually. In many cases, removing the upper inch or two of soil and replacing it with highly enriched soil will suffice. This method of handling is often used with plants grown in tubs and other large containers which are difficult to handle because of their weight and size.

WASHING

Keep the leaves of plants clean. Dust settling on the leaves not only detracts from the appearance of the plants but also jeopardizes their health, because it closes their breathing pores.

Plants with large flat leaves, like sansevierias, rubber plants and rex begonias, can be sponged off with a damp cloth. Other plants can be syringed.

TEMPERATURE AND HUMIDITY

As mentioned before, most of our homes are too hot for the best growth of plants during the winter months. A cool room, where the temperature runs from 60 to 70 degrees, will suit most plants better than a higher temperature. Most plants resent being subjected to sudden changes in temperature. Some of them show it by a yellowing of the leaves, while others will stop flowering when they are thoroughly chilled.

If the air in your home is dry, as it is in most modern houses in winter, syringing the foliage of the plants every few days will help most of them. An atomizer is ideal for this purpose. Pans of wet peat or sphagnum moss placed among the plants will also furnish much-needed moisture.

SUMMER CARE

Except for the dwarf and fragile species, many of the plants will do better if you plunge the pots into the earth outdoors in a shady place for the summer. They do not dry out so badly when the pots are buried in the soil, and the sunlight and air tend to harden the plants and give them more stamina. I don't mean that you should place the plants outdoors and forget all about them; it will be necessary to continue regular watering and feeding. With the first suggestion of chilly nights in the fall, lift the pots carefully and bring them indoors.

28

Potpourri

MOISTURE IN THE GARDEN

Horticultural plants have a circulatory system quite unlike that of the human body. It does not form an endless chain. The water in the soil which contains minerals and nutrients in solution is taken up by the roots of the plants and passes up through the stems to the leaves, where the minute food factories are situated. Any excess moisture is lost through transpiration, a term used to cover the loss of moisture through the leaves in the form of vapor.

Nutrients of any kind must be reduced to liquid form before they can be utilized by the plant. Many plants lose a surprisingly large quantity of water in the process of transpiration. Large-leaved plants like the candelabra, castor bean, or sunflower can lose from a pint to a quart of water on a bright, hot summer day. It is said that a full-grown heavy-foliaged live oak or red oak may lose anywhere from 20,000 to 30,000 gallons of water during one of our long summer seasons.

Water loss through transpiration must be replaced either by rainfall or by artificial means. Otherwise the plants will suffer and may finally die. Many plants wilt when they run short of moisture. Scientists say that this is a process activated by nature to stop transpiration when the moisture supply begins to run too low.

Heavy-foliaged plants require lots of water while the lightly foliaged ones where the transpiration is light require a much lesser amount.

Of course, no one can tell precisely how much water a given plant or flower bed will need, but we can learn a great deal from watching our plants under average cultural conditions. Most gardeners in the South make the common mistake of watering too lightly. They sprinkle a little water on the beds, which may revive the plants but does not entirely quench their thirst. Merely wetting the upper quarter inch of soil may do far more harm than good. Many times it results in the feed roots turning upward toward the surface, and these plants may suffer severely during hot dry periods. When water is applied at all, enough should be given not only to reach the area where the roots are growing but much deeper to encourage a downward growth of the root system.

Some years ago I experimented with several beds of annual flowers, sprinkling them lightly every day but never thoroughly soaking the beds. After a few weeks I found that if the beds did not get this daily sprinkling the plants would wilt by early afternoon. An examination revealed that many of the roots had actually come to the very surface and were uncovered when the hose was turned on the bed. On another bed where an inch of water was applied once a week, the roots were several inches under the surface and the plants never showed any indication of suffering from the lack of moisture.

In the latitude of Meridian, Mississippi, the annual rainfall is about 53 inches per year, which gives us an average of approximately one inch per week. Of course, in the hot dry summers, plant life can use much more than this average, while in the cloudy, cooler winters they may need much less.

I am told that this 53-inch average holds for a belt running across the entire South about 150 miles from the Gulf Coast. Approaching the Coast the rainfall is slightly heavier, while in the Upper South it would probably be slightly lighter.

When watering lawns, let the sprinkler run in the same spot until it has discharged about an inch of water. A good practice is to rotate the use of the sprinkler from spot to spot, day by day, in such a way that the entire lawn would be covered in one week.

Of course, we can use too much water, especially in a location where water tends to collect or where the drainage is not good. While water is essential for the healthy growth of plants, too much of it can be harmful. Air cannot penetrate soils that are filled with water, and plant life may actually die if it is kept in an over-wet condition too long. So try to give enough water but be careful not to give too much.

Except for those plants susceptible to fungus diseases, which develop more rapidly when the plants are wet, it is better to water the garden in the late afternoon. At the end of the day the temperature is lower and there will be less evaporation; the plants will receive a greater benefit from the water applied.

Sprinkling the foliage of many shrubs in the late afternoon, including azaleas, camellias and gardenias, tends to revive them and enable them to go through hot weather in better condition. I must make it clear, however, that this sprinkling of the foliage does not take the place of adequate watering at the roots.

Shrubs and young trees that have been growing in their present locations for only a season or two may suffer from lack of moisture and should be carefully watched to see that they get all the moisture they need. This applies especially to shallow-rooted shrubs such as azaleas and camellias.

You will find a number of devices at the garden stores that will probably aid you in applying water more efficiently. Soil soakers made of narrow, long canvas bags to which the hose can be attached are fine for watering the lawn and flower beds. During the last few years there have been placed on the market several types of perforated garden hose which are excellent for watering. When placed face down they water only a very narrow strip, but if turned face up they can sprinkle the flower bed up to eight or ten feet or more, depending on the amount of pressure supplied by the water faucet. If you will place a bread pan or other flat container out on the lawn within the range of the sprinkler, you will probably find that it requires much longer to catch an inch of water than you think.

MULCHES

In the South we could not very well garden without mulches. A good mulch is one of the best means of preventing the loss of moisture from the earth and of keeping down weeds. Not only will it reduce the amount of artificial watering usually required but it keeps the earth cool and protects shallow-rooted plants from the heat of the summer sun and from freezes during the winter.

Mulches decay and add much fertility and friability to the soil as well. There are, of course, exceptions to all rules, and in garden practice we find that a few plants do better without a mulch.

Bearded irises and members of the daisy family seem to do better without any mulch whatever. Long-growing perennials and annuals like cosmoses, chrysanthemums, roses, sunflowers and begonias particularly like the protection offered by a good mulch. Mulches are considered "musts" for azaleas, camellias and rhododendrons.

For acid-loving plants, peat moss, oak leaves and pine needles make very satisfactory mulches. Other good mulching materials include cottonseed hulls, hay, straw, leaves of various kinds, lawn clippings (when not left on the lawn) and waste from cottonseed-oil mills.

I have used black mulching paper very successfully in the culture of chrysanthemums, dahlias and roses and some other things that are grown in rows. While it may last only a single season, black building paper, which can be secured from building supply concerns, makes a very good mulch.

GARDENING WITHOUT WEEDS

Several years ago when garden labor became rather difficult to find and competent garden help was not available at any price, I reached the conclusion that it would be necessary for gardeners everywhere to find a substitute for the great amount of weed pulling, hoeing and cultivation that had been routine for every gardener.

This was at a time when chemical weed killers of various kinds were just beginning to be used in the cultivation of farm crops, and I found ample chemicals for keeping down the weeds of large cotton, corn and soy bean plantations, but even the U. S. Department of Agriculture experiment stations did not seem to know too much about the use of chemicals in the vegetable and flower gardens at that time.

Unlike most of the chemicals then being used for the control of weeds in field crops, those used for the flower garden would have to be largely of the pre-emergent type so as not to injure the flowers already growing in the garden.

I began a program of experimentation on my own and found only a few pre-emergent killers on the market at that time. I found the manufacturers of these weed controllers very coopera-tive, and they supplied, without cost, ample material for my experiments. As time went by I found available more prepara-tions designed and packaged for use by the home gardener.

The several products which I tested gave highly satisfactory results. One application made about the first of March, and an-other about the last of April, practically eliminated all weed pulling from my daylily garden and other areas where only perennial flowers are grown.

These pre-emergent killers are effective only while the weed seeds are in process of germination and will have no effect on weeds, grass and flowers already growing in the area. As used in my daylily garden, which is largely devoted to hybridizing and breeding daylilies, I encountered practically no weeds at all. Some gardeners consider these chemicals a bit expensive, but in view of the considerable amount of hoeing and weed pulling that they save, I consider them a great bargain for both the flower and vegetable gardens.

The products which I have used do not require incorporation into the soil, which would be impractical in areas where plants are already growing. They are merely sprinkled over the soil or sprayed on the surface according to directions. I have always followed the policy of wetting down with the hose after the chemicals are applied, but I am told that this is not really necessary.

There are several pre-emergent killers available. Your garden store manager or county agent should be able to advise you as to the proper one for your particular use. Judging from the results of my several years of tests in which I used several check plots, their use will become very wide in the next few years.

In many cases if we can keep the weeds out for two successive seasons there will not be very many seeds left in the soil to annoy us with new weeds for several seasons.

GIBBING

It was 1958 when I had my first experience in the use of gibberellic acid, or gibbing, as the practice is widely called. The chemical had been isolated about two years before that time, but enough of the product had to become available to supply both the research men and individual gardeners.

During the intervening years much has been learned in connection with the use of this acid in the culture of ornamental plants of various genera. A wide variety of uses on a wide range of plants has been found, but here in the Deep South it seems that its most popular use at present is for forcing earlier bloom on *Camellia japonica* and for increasing the size of bloom as well.

How does the gibbing on horticultural plants generally act? Usually the first and most obvious effect is the lengthening of the internodes, or distance between leaf buds. This results in remarkable growth in some species of plants but very little in others. The early research showed that in a given time, used on a given plant, the use of the chemical caused the individual cells to elongate, rather than stimulating the development of more cells. The elongated cells caused the plants to grow taller, which explains the amazing height of some plants after a few applica tions of the acid.

Reports indicated that applications of the chemical resulted in many annuals and perennials, in addition to camellias, flowering earlier and giving much larger flowers. One of the very remarkable results, according to one report, was that it caused some fruits, including cucumbers, tomatoes and eggplants, to fruit without pollen. Fruit so produced is usually seedless but otherwise normal.

Gibbing does not seem to stimulate root growth to the same extent that it does leaf growth. In several tests made in the early days of its use on horticultural plants where roots were measured and weighed, the weight and size of the roots in the treated plots were the same or even a bit under those of the untreated areas.

There seems to be much about the use of these acids that we do not yet know. The response is not always just what is expected. The results may vary with different species. Age of the plant, temperature and length of day all seem to have some weight.

Ageratum plants when treated showed increased length of laterals, dahlias flowered earlier, geraniums grew taller and had larger blooms, hydrangeas made faster stem growth, begonias grew taller and were more uniform in bloom, poinsettias grew taller, petunias bloomed earlier with heavier crops of flowers, roses grew faster, snapdragons and stocks bloomed earlier with heavier crops of flowers and marigolds and zinnias grew taller.

The reports stated that there was a marked response in treated boxwoods, citrus trees, junipers, maples and oaks, all of which showed longer stems and more lateral branches. On most pines there was very little response.

The treatment of dormant bulbs and roots of potatoes, dahlias and onions did not seem to affect the growth of these plants to any noticeable degree, but applications on the growing plants resulted in a marked increase in stem growth.

In the early years of its use on garden plants only concentrated acid was sold, but now at the garden stores you should be able to find formulations ready for application, saving the tedious chore of dilution. While the safety factor is large, over-dosage could easily injure plants; for this reason, directions should be strictly followed in the use of these chemicals.

The report is based on information obtained from sources considered reliable, but we must admit that our personal use of this acid during the early years was disappointing—we simply did not get anything approaching the results claimed by so many others. But further use over a period of years has convinced us that it has a tremendous potential. Right now, it seems to me, its most promising results stem from its use on outdoor-grown *Camellia japonica*, to bring these plants into bloom much earlier than their normal season and enable us to enjoy them before they are cut down by the freezes. And it also results in much, much larger flowers.

At the very least, we will have to admit that this is an interesting chemical and is worth the attention of all serious gardeners.

KEEPING CUT FLOWERS FRESH

The length of life of cut flowers is almost always of very great importance, regardless of whether they are for home decoration or for exhibiting in a show. If we buy them at the flower shop, we are disappointed if they fade away at once; if we cut them from our own beds for home decoration, we want them to last as long as possible; and if they are for exhibition it is all important that they maintain a fresh, newly cut look, at least until after they have been judged.

In recent years we have learned much about keeping flowers fresh. Modern science has shown us improved methods and many ways in which to better our practices. Chemical formulas have been perfected that will, when added to the water in which they are placed, add greatly to the life of cut flowers, in some cases actually doubling their life.

It will help to know something of the flowers we are using and to modify our system of handling to meet the requirements of each particular species. Most annual flowers differ from the bulbous and perennial types in that after they are cut the stems rarely have the ability to continue development so that the tight flower buds will unfold. The tight bud of the zinnia will never open after the stem has been cut; but in the case of the gladiolus, if the tight lower florets are showing color, practically every flower bud on the stem can be counted on to open into a good flower. A good rule, then, in cutting annuals, is to select newly opened blooms and not depend on tight or unopened buds.

I learned from consulting several different sources that authorities do not agree on the best time of day to cut flowers. The exact time, I think, differs with the species, and perhaps with the variety of flower; but speaking generally, I think we can assume that flowers with hollow stems like calendulas and zinnias will keep best if cut in the afternoon when the plants are in a slightly wilted condition. This sounded like stark heresy when I first heard it, as I had always been taught that all flowers should be cut in the early morning when fresh with dew. But the hollow-stemmed types, when cut in the afternoon—just a bit limp but not too wilted, of course—will take up water rapidly.

After cutting, do not let them wilt further but plunge them deep into water just as soon as you can and keep them in a cool place overnight. In the morning you will probably find that both stems and flowers have plumped up amazingly. With stiff stems and perky flowers you can go ahead and make your arrangements. Some prominent arrangers who advocate this system even claim that it is better to cut the flowers a full day in advance, chilling them overnight and keeping them in a cool place until used. This would keep them fresh for arrangements used in the evening.

But many flowers have solid stems, so read on, please. Flowers with solid stems like cosmoses and poppies should be cut in the morning just after the flowers have opened. The solid stems are slow in taking up moisture, so it is wise to pick them before their supply of moisture has been depleted by transpiration, sun, heat and wind.

Stems of poppies, poinsettias and others that "bleed" when

cut should be dipped in very hot water to a depth of about an inch before being placed in their containers of water. Or you may sear the stems over a candle or other small flame.

Some flowers, for reasons which I shall not attempt to explain here, are not adapted to use as cut flowers. You rarely see baby blue-eyes (nemophila), liatris, brown-eyed Susan, certain types of morning glory or nicotiana used in arrangements. Sometimes we overlook some of the common flowers that are very good for cutting. Most of the new petunias make glowing attractions for the coffee table, dining table or mantel; the new marigolds and zinnias, of course, are first-rate material.

New preservatives are coming into the market from time to time, so talk to your florist—he may have something that is particularly suited to your needs. But even with the new chemicals and improved methods, we will have to do a little more, in the Deep South, in order to have fresh flowers all through the blooming season. To have fresh flowers during parts of the late summer and fall, we will have to make additional plantings. Most of the hot-weather annuals will reach maturity, finish blooming and begin to fade out by June or July. We can greatly lengthen the season of some of them by keeping faded flowers removed regularly, pruning the plants back lightly, feeding them well and keeping them supplied with moisture during the dry season.

FUNCTION OF PLANT FOODS

In the South most gardeners fail to grasp the importance of plant food. They fail to realize fully that all plant life, as well as animal life, must have food in order to survive. Under normal conditions nearly all soils in the South contain a certain amount of plant food, but most of them are deficient in certain elements to the extent that we find it necessary to apply additional fertilizers at regular intervals if we wish to attain satisfactory growth, bloom and fruit.

Ornamental plants as well as others use numerous elements in their growth and development. These include carbon, calcium, magnesium, potassium, nitrogen, phosphorus, silicon and sulphur—and there may be several others. Most of these, however, are what is called trace elements and are found in most soils in sufficient quantity to supply the plants' needs.

There are three of these elements, however, nitrogen, phosphate (phosphorus) and potash (potassium), which are usually in short supply and will have to be added to most soils in order to get satisfactory results. These three elements form the base of most commercial fertilizers, and the quantity of each is always shown in the analysis of the plant food. The first figure in the combination indicates the nitrogen, the second the amount of phosphate, and the third or last the amount of potash present. A plant food showing an analysis of 6–8–8 would contain 6 percent nitrogen and 8 percent each of phosphate and potash. Most commercial plant foods contain at least these three basic elements and are therefore called "complete" fertilizers.

Of all the elements in the complete plant foods, nitrogen is perhaps the most important. Its chief function is to stimulate growth; if it is not present in sufficient quantity, the plant does not show the usual desirable dark green color, luxuriant foliage and internodes or sections of proper length between leaves. If too much nitrogen is present there may be excess sappy growth that is easily damaged by drought, cold or hot weather.

The term "super phosphate" is sometimes used to describe phosphorus. This element has much to do with the blooming and fruiting of plants. It gives strength and sturdiness to stems and flowers.

Potash is related to the formation and transfer of sugar, starch and other compounds used in the structure of plants. It gives strength and stability to leaf and stem; it is particularly important in the life of tuberous plants like potatoes, dahlias and bulbs. A lack of potash affects the vitality of a plant.

The cost of commercial fertilizers usually depends largely on the amount of nitrogen they contain. For instance, a fertilizer that contains 20 percent nitrogen should be expected to cost about twice as much as one that contains 10 percent.

The amount of nitrogen determines in a large measure how much fertilizer is to be applied. A popular formula used on the farms of the South, and also on vegetable and flower gardens, is 6–8–8. If your fertilizer is based on a formula containing about twice as much nitrogen, 12–10–12 for example, you would only use about half as much for a given area as you would of 6–8–8.

It should be pointed out that fertilizer cannot be utilized by the plant in dry form and must be converted to liquid form before it can be taken up by the plant roots. Plant food in liquid form gives much quicker results in cases where there is immediate need.

I am a strong advocate of the use of adequate fertilizer, and on small plants, like annuals and perennials, the liquid form seems to be preferable. All plant food, whether liquid or dry, should be used strictly according to directions put out by the manufacturer.

PLANT SPORTS AND MUTATIONS

The announcement by a world-renowned seedsman and hybridist of an offer of $10,000 for a pure white marigold meeting certain specifications is a common subject of discussion among gardeners all over the country. When one thinks of the vast amount of research done by the hybridists and the great improvement made by them in marigolds, zinnias and many other flowers, he is inclined to suggest that a white marigold is not too far away.

The scientists have done much to improve our various garden plants. Many of the colorful species which adorn our gardens today were insignificant woodland plants of doubtful value a few generations ago. Yet many of the outstanding and spectacular developments in plant life have not been achieved by scientific researchers but by a peculiar quirk of nature no one of us is quite able to explain. When the Burpees decided they must have a scentless marigold, they did not depend on their scientists, geneticists and hybridists; they sent scores of boys and girls into the acres of marigold fields. Crawling along the rows, pinching and smelling the leaves, these youngsters finally ran across one that did not smell. Nature did the job for them.

When the white marigold is finally achieved, I'm placing my

bets on Nature to do the job; it will be a sport of a plant producing flowers of another color—maybe lemon or yellow. The word "sport," as most of us know, is a term applied to an abrupt deviation from type—scientifically, a mutation. There may be a small branch on a plant which produces flowers of a color entirely different from those on the remainder of the plant. Sports are many times found on camellias, carnations, azaleas, roses and some other plants.

As a rule these sports gladden the heart of the nurseryman and plant propagator, as Nature throws something in his lap that he sometimes works for many years to achieve and which even then may elude him. Some years ago a friend in Tyler, Texas, who grows roses commercially was walking through a field of President Hoovers and found a plant with one small branch bearing rosy-red flowers—and the Texas Centennial was born. From this little branch he took buds and started propagation of the new variety. Down in Florida some years ago pink-colored sports were found on plants of Formosa azaleas, and from them we have the varieties Judge Solomon and Southern Charm.

Many of the popular camellias are sports. C. M. Wilson is a pink sport of the popular Elegans, while High Hat is a sport of Daikagura. Many years ago the Department of Agriculture imported a few plants of Chinese holly (*Ilex cornuta*), one of which was sent to Atlanta, Georgia, for test growing. The superintendent of the cemetery where the plant was growing, a Mr. Burford, discovered a branch that was practically spineless. It was used for propagation, and now we have the popular Burford holly.

Nature is no respecter of persons when it comes to producing sports on plants. You are just as likely to find one in your own backyard garden as the keeper of a great estate, but of course the greater the number of plants you grow the greater your chances of a lucky find. Your sport or mutation may not be superior to the mother plant, but if there is a noticeable difference in foliage, color or form of flower it would be well to propagate it.

Of course, most new varieties of garden flowers are produced from seed grown in hybridizing. Most of our new camellias, daylilies, irises, roses and many others are grown from seed produced by crossing different types. Most annual flowers are fixed in type and will come true from seed, but named varieties of perennial plants are naturally propagated from some sort of division of the mother plant.

FLOWERING TREES

Landscape authorities tell us that much care should be used in selecting trees for the home grounds. The size and shape of the house, its location on the lot and proximity to other structures, as well as the matter of shade and sunlight, should be given consideration when we plan our tree planting.

Some situations, especially those on small city lots, may not provide adequate space for the average- or large-growing tree. These problems may be met by the use of the smaller-growing flowering trees, which may be used on both the large grounds and very small ones. The foliage of these small trees furnishes needed shade in spring and summer, and in autumn the leaves of many species turn to brilliant hues, adding much color to the landscape. Their flowers in spring and summer can transform a drab situation into one of great charm and beauty. No building lot is too large or too small for at least a few of these smaller-growing trees.

Practically all genera of trees produce flowers of one sort or another, but there is one group, usually small in growth, that is so conspicuous when in flower that they are commonly called "flowering trees." In the colder areas there has long been wide use of these small trees in landscape beautification, but here in the South we have given them very little attention until the last few years. Right now, however, they are being rather widely planted, especially the crab apples.

During my early years of gardening, the only flowering crab found on local markets (nurseries and sales yards) was the lovely double-flowering Bechtel, but we soon learned, much to our sorrow, that on account of cedar-apple rust it could not be grown in close proximity to the common red cedars, with which many home grounds abounded. Then we tried the native crabs, but they did no better than the Bechtel. No amount of spraying with the best-known fungicides seemed to help.

We have always considered the crab as one of our loveliest flowering trees, and were delighted when a friend told us that the Hopa variety was immune to cedar-apple rust and scab. We planted one which is now ten years old and have another one that is only half as old. Both have, so far, proved immune to both these diseases. The Hopa is rather large-growing for a crab, and ours did not bloom well until it was three or four years old, but since that age it has given a great display of bloom each spring. With its bronze foliage and rose-pink flowers it always attracts much attention. The flowers are followed with red fruits which hang on until late fall.

We have two plants each of Almey and Eley, all of which are growing nicely and have shown no symptoms of disease. The blooms of Almey are supposed to be red, but ours are pink; while those of Eley are a pinkish white.

We also have a nice young plant of Katherine, which is a semi-double light pink. I consider it one of the prettiest of all the crabs. Last spring our plant, as well as that of a neighbor, showed signs of fire blight, but after the diseased branches were removed the disease did not reappear. Katherine appears to be a very dwarf form and can be used either as a specimen or on the shrub border.

A few years ago I saw at the Callaway Garden Center in Jackson, Mississippi, a very lovely crab in full bloom, but no one there was able to identify it as to variety. It was later identified, I understand, as *Malus floribunda* or Japanese crab. The Floribunda is an old variety but does not seem to be widely grown in the South. The character of growth, size and color of bloom closely resemble the native form so abundant in the pine hill sections of the South. The large flower buds are a deep pink but open into white blooms. A well-developed plant carrying an abundance of both buds and flowers is a beautiful thing to see. It is said to be relatively immune to both scab and rust.

Except in the South, the "flowering" or cultivated crab has long been a popular ornamental, especially for small home grounds. Now many Southern home owners are recognizing the many merits of these lovely little trees and are planting more of them. In addition to the beauty of the flowers, many of the crabs bear edible fruits that may be utilized in making jams and jellies.

You will probably not find a great number of varieties at any one garden store or nursery in this area. Before buying I suggest you make inquiry about the plants' susceptibility to diseases.

As with most flowering trees, we get the greatest beauty from the crabs when they are given ample space to develop along natural lines on all sides. If crowded for space, these trees will develop a poor form and the flowers will be few as compared to a tree that has full room for development.

WHEN PLANTS NEED A DOCTOR

Plants, like human beings, occasionally get sick. And, as in the case of humans, if the doctor is called in time a prolonged illness or death usually can be prevented.

Where human beings are concerned, good health practices call for a complete check-up at regular intervals to make sure that no unsuspected trouble has developed. The same thing applies to ornamental plants. At regular intervals, check each bed, shrub and tree—especially the valuable ones—noting the quality and extent of new growth and the color of the foliage. Examine the undersides of the leaves for insect infestation.

Sometimes a physician is called in to see a patient, only to find that the basic trouble is simple malnutrition. Garden plants often suffer from the same cause. Professional plant doctors tell us that many fatal plant diseases get a foothold solely because the "patient" has been weakened by lack of food and moisture. If your plants appear to be unhealthy, check their nutrition first. Make sure that your diet list provides for properly balanced food and adequate moisture. When plants are well nourished, many cases of apparent illness soon disappear.

If you keep close watch over your plants, it is easy to recognize the difference between a healthy, thrifty specimen and a sick one. In the process of cultivating, feeding, watering and mulching, you become acquainted with your plants and learn to recognize full vigorous growth in each particular kind.

The plant doctor—and in most cases you are the doctor—should first of all be able to diagnose the trouble. It is impossible to treat a plant disease successfully unless you understand its cause; treatment based on faulty diagnosis is not only useless but hazardous.

Many illnesses are easy to diagnose, while the symptoms of others are not so easily recognized. Take the leading rose disease, for example. Most of us know that irregular dark spots with yellow margins found on the leaves are symptoms of the fungus disease called black spot, which can be checked by the use of any good fungicide, either dust or spray.

If the tops of your azalea leaves look frosty, as though they were covered with a grayish mildew, examine the undersides; if you see a reddish varnishlike substance, you doubtless have azalea lace bugs. They can cause your plants to look as though they are already halfway to the graveyard and will so devitalize them that both growth and bloom will be unsatisfactory. Any good insecticide applied in March and again in September will usually completely clear the plants.

Gardenias that have been neglected sometimes show a black sooty substance on the tops of the leaves. When this is present you will usually find undeveloped insects in various stages of growth on the undersides of the leaves. This situation may be caused by either soft scale or white flies, or by the two attacking at the same time. The insects leave a sweet substance on the leaves in which a fungus growth sets up, causing the sooty appearance. Here again, a reliable pesticide will check the insects, but several sprayings at monthly intervals may be required.

Camellias will do their best to let you know when they are attacked by scale. While the insects do their damage from the undersides of the leaves, their dirty work is indicated by pale yellow spots on the upper surfaces. If you see these spots, be sure to look under the leaves; if you find scale (it may be either hard or soft), wash it off with a soft cloth and soapy water. Then, when the plants are dry, spray them with an oil-base solution.

If close check of your roses shows that some buds "ball" and do not open, the mischief is probably caused by thrips. Pull off one of the balled flowers and carefully pull it apart. If thrips are present, you will see them running around in a great hurry at the base of the petals. They move fast, so you'll have to look quickly to see them. Thrips also attack chrysanthemums, causing them to ball in the same way. As a protection against these insects, spray the tops of the plants with insecticide at ten-day intervals for several weeks prior to the opening of the first blooms.

Nearly every gardener has had the disheartening experience of going out early in the morning to see how the seedlings of petunias, asters and various other plants are coming along, only to find that many of them have been eaten off just above the ground. This is the work of cutworms, slugs, snails and sow bugs, all of which can be controlled by using one of the prepared remedies found at the stores.

Whether it is insects or disease that is causing trouble in your garden, early diagnosis is vitally important. And prompt treatment can forestall an "epidemic" which could wipe out the whole planting.

When I first began preparation of this book, a few years ago, it was my intention to make specific recommendations for the control of all common insects and diseases of the flower garden, but such a strong protest has developed against the use of certain insecticides and their influence on the ecology of the country, and so many changes have been made in recommendations in recent months, that I now hesitate to make specific suggestions for the control of any insect or disease.

The situation is still fluid, and chemicals are being banned at a rapid rate. Any recommendation that I might make as this is written could easily be nullified by new federal orders issued before the book appears in print.

In chapters devoted to single ornamental flowers or classes of ornamentals, I gave, in most cases, recommendations for control of pests of that particular group. I shall give here only some general suggestions, several of which have been excerpted from a bulletin prepared by J. E. Brogdon, L. C. Kuitert and S. H. Kerr, all well-known and highly regarded entomologists at the University of Florida, and issued by the Florida Cooperative Extension Service. The bulletin suggests, among other things:

To combat insect pests successfully, something should be known about the manner in which they develop and feed. Insects normally hatch from eggs deposited on or near the food supply; although in some cases they hatch within the female's body, and active young emerge from the female. Adults are usually individuals with fully developed wings, although a few species of insects never have wings. Insects pass through several stages during their development. Plant bugs, leafhoppers, thrips, and grasshoppers hatch from the egg in a form known as a nymph. The nymph resembles the full-grown insect, except that it lacks wings and is smaller. It sheds its skin periodically as it gradually increases in size. Moths, beetles, and flies, on the other hand, hatch from the eggs as a worm-like form, or larva, much different from the adult. The larva of a moth or butterfly is commonly called a caterpillar, the larva of a beetle is called a grub, and the larva of a fly is known as maggot. Larvae also molt, or shed their skins periodically, and in growing to full size, change to an inactive form, which is known as pupa. The adult insect emerges from this pupa. The length of life varies greatly with different species of insects. Some develop from egg to adult in a few weeks, many require a year, and a few take two or more years to reach maturity.

Pests of ornamentals may be divided into two groups by the way they feed.

a. *Insects with chewing mouthparts.* They bite off and swallow portions of the plant. They may eat the leaves and flowers, bore into the stems, or feed on the roots. Examples are: Caterpillars, beetles, grasshoppers, katydids.

b. *Pests with piercing-sucking mouthparts.* They have beak-like mouthparts, which are used for piercing the plant tissue and sucking the plant juices. Examples are: Scales, aphids, white-flies, mealybugs, stink bugs, and mites.

Chemical Control. Insecticides are required to control insects and related pests on many ornamental plants. Most of the newer insecticides kill by contact with the insect or as a stomach poison. Some also exert a fumigating or vapor action under certain conditions. Materials should be selected that will be effective in controlling the pests without injuring the plant, or causing build-up of other pests.

    a. Select the right material.
    b. Apply it at the right time.
    c. Use the right amount.
    d. Apply it in the right way.

General-purpose sprays for control of insects and mites. Needless to say, it is impossible to suggest one spray mixture that will control all insects and mite pests of ornamentals. It will often be necessary to make additional treatments with other insecticides for certain pests. . . . General-purpose sprays are commercially available at the garden stores.

Systemic insecticides. A systemic insecticide is a chemical compound that is absorbed by the insect host, translocated throughout its tissues, and makes the host toxic to certain insect pests. Several systemic insecticides are absorbed by growing plants. Some are taken up from the soil by the roots of the plants and translocated throughout the plant tissues; others can be absorbed by foliage or stem sprays or injections into the plants.

Systemic insecticides have been effective primarily against small sucking insects including aphids, whiteflies, scales, mealybugs, and spider mites. In general, they have not given satisfactory control of chewing insect pests.

[Some] systemic insecticides are available as emulsifiable concentrates for use by home gardeners as well as commercial growers. They can be mixed with water and applied as foliar sprays. [Some may] be applied as a soil drench. Sprays give quicker kill, but the residual effect on insects is much shorter than soil drenches.

Systemic insecticides applied to the soil as drenches or granules have been more effective against insects on container-grown plants than on field-grown plants.

. . . Systemic insecticides are available in different formulations and concentrations and the amounts may vary with different ornamental plants. *Follow the directions and cautions on the manufacturer's container label for the amounts to use on the ornamental plants specified on the label.*

Safety precautions:

a. All insecticides are poisons, and the safety precautions on the container labels should be followed.
b. Read the entire label, including the small print, before opening the container.
c. Store pesticides in their original labelled containers out of the reach of children, irresponsible people, and pets, and preferably keep under lock and key.
d. Dispose of left-over spray materials and empty containers promptly and safely.
e. Keep pesticides from getting into fish ponds, streams, and water supplies.
f. Avoid drift of pesticides to adjacent areas or to crops that may be eaten by man or animals.

Since the term "ecology" has come into such common use and the media have been filled with the subject of environmental danger, I have made inquiry of the agricultural departments of several of our Southern universities. I have also interviewed practical gardeners in different sections of the South, and the proprietors of local plant stores, and I do not find any recommendations for the use of chemicals that are currently barred for use in home gardens. It was found that, as a rule, extension services do not recommend trade-named products but rather an individual pesticide for each pest. This sometimes makes it difficult and expensive, for the home gardener may not feel he can afford to buy a dozen different insecticides and fungicides to control as many insects and diseases. While I have no desire or intention to question the advice and recommendations of the learned entomologists of our universities, I have found through many years of home gardening that a general-purpose spray as suggested by the University of Florida scientists just quoted will take care of the control of practically all insects of the average Southern garden. Consult your county agent and seed stores and be sure to observe the safety precautions mentioned; also make sure that the product you plan to use has not been barred by the federal authorities.

Appendixes

GLOSSARY

The first word in a botanical scientific name (which usually consists of two or more words) is the generic name, which is common to the entire genus. The second word in the name is usually the specific name; it may describe some characteristics of the species, as in *Magnolia macrophyllus,* where "macrophyllus" indicates that the species has large leaves, or it may be geographical, as in *Quercus japonica,* where the "japonica" indicates that the species came from Japan.

A knowledge of the species or meaning of the descriptive name is of great importance to the average gardener, as he frequently encounters them in the garden and also in garden literature. We submit a brief list of the Latin terms commonly used in horticultural literature in the hope that it will prove helpful and interesting.

acaulis: stemless
acidus: acid
acuminatus: acuminate, tapering
acutus: sharp-pointed
adpressus: pressed down
africanus: African
albus: white
altus: tall
amabilis: lovely
americanus: American
anacanthus: spineless
angularis: angular
angustus: narrow
apetalus: without petals
aphyllus: leafless

arborescens: treelike
aureus: golden
australis: southern
autumnalis: autumnal
baccatus: berried
barbatus: barbed
bicolor: two-colored
biennis: biennial—living only two years
bonus: good
botryoides: clusterlike
brevis: short
bulbosus: bulbous
canadensis: Canadian
candicans: white
candidus: white

cardinalis: cardinal
carolinianus: relating to the Carolinas
chinensis: Chinese
clandestinus: concealed
coccineus: scarlet
communis: common
compactus: compact
compressus: compressed
concolor: similarly colored
conifera: cone-bearing
conspicuus: conspicuous
deciduus: deciduous
decorus: elegant, comely
deflexus: deflexed
depressus: depressed
digitatus: digitate
flavus: yellow
foetidus: bad-smelling
fragrans: fragrant
fulvus: fulvous
glabratus: smooth
gladiatus: swordlike
gracillis: graceful
grandiflorus: large-flowered
helianthoides: sunflowerlike
incomparabilis: incomparable
japonicus: Japanese
kewensis: from Kew Gardens (England)
lactatus: milky
lanatus: woolly
lancifolius: lance-leaved
latifolius: broad-leaved
leucophyllus: white-leaved
lucidus: bright, shining
macranthus: large-flowered

macrophyllus: large-leaved
maximus: largest
micranthus: small-flowered
microphyllus: small-leaved
millefolius: thousand-leaved
niger: black
nigratus: blackish
oblongus: oblong
occidentalis: western
palmatus: palmate, divided like the hand
parviflorus: small-flowered
pennatus: feathered, pinnate
perennis: living three or more years
pinifolius: pine-leaved
pinnatus: pinnate, leaflets on the sides of a main axis
planus: planelike, flat
plumarius: plumed
plumosus: feathery
polygamus: polygamous, having both perfect and imperfect flowers
procumbens: procumbent, lying down
prostratus: prostrate
pubescens: downy, pubescent
pulcher: handsome
pumilus: dwarf
pungens: piercing, sharp-pointed
purpureus: purple
quercinus: oaklike
quinatus: in fives
quinquecolor: five-colored

quinqueflorus: five-flowered
quinquefolius: five-leaved
racemosus: flowers in racemes
radiatus: radiate, rayed
rectus: upright
reptans: creeping
rotundifolius: round-leaved
saccharatus: containing sugar
saxatilis: found among rocks
sempervirens: evergreen
serratus: serrate, saw-toothed
silvestris: relating to the woods, sylvan
spectabilis: spectacular
splendens: splendid
stellatus: stellate, starry
taxifolius: yew-leaved
tenuifolius: slender-leaved

tomentosus: tomentose, pubescent
tricolor: three-colored
triflorus: three-flowered
trifolius: three-leaved
trivialis: common, ordinary
undulatus: undulated, wavy
unicolor: one-colored
uniflorus: one-flowered
virens: green
virginalis: virgin
virginicus: Virginian
viridifolius: green-leaved
viridis: green
vulgatus: common
xanthocarpus: yellow-fruited
yunnanensis: from Yunnan (China)

FREE HELP

There is no end to the number of helpful leaflets, booklets and bulletins treating on the culture of plants that may be obtained from the U.S. Department of Agriculture, the state experiment stations and other sources. You may have to ask for it through your congressman, but it is prepared at public expense and if you do not get your share of it you are short-changed. To receive garden help, make requests to your local extension service repre sentatives. Their offices are normally located at the county court-houses. Invariably you will find these public employees knowl-edgeable and glad to be of service.

At the state level you should be able to obtain valuable in-formation and assistance from the agricultural extension service of your particular state. These services for various Southern states are located as follows:

Alabama: Auburn University, Auburn, Alabama 36833
Arkansas: University of Arkansas, Fayetteville, Arkansas 72701

Florida: University of Florida, Gainesville, Florida 32601
Georgia: University of Georgia, Athens, Georgia 30601
Kentucky: College of Agriculture, Lexington, Kentucky 40500
Louisiana: Louisiana State University, Baton Rouge, Louisiana 70800
Mississippi: Mississippi State University, State College, Mississippi 39762
New Mexico: State College of Agriculture, Los Cruces, New Mexico 88001
North Carolina: State College of Agriculture, Raleigh, North Carolina 27600
Oklahoma: A & M College, Stillwater, Oklahoma 74074
South Carolina: Clemson College, Clemson, South Carolina 29631
Tennessee: University of Tennessee, Knoxville, Tennessee 37900
Texas: A & M College, College Station, Texas 77840
Virginia: A & M College, Blacksburg, Virginia 24060
West Virginia: State College, Morgantown, West Virginia 26501

STATE FLOWERS

Alabama: Camellia
Alaska: Forget-me-not
Arizona: Saguaro
Arkansas: Apple blossom
California: California poppy
Colorado: Columbine
Connecticut: Mountain laurel
Delaware: Peach blossom
District of Columbia: American Beauty rose
Florida: Orange blossom
Georgia: Cherokee rose
Hawaii: Hibiscus
Idaho: Syringa
Illinois: Wood violet
Indiana: Peony

Iowa: Wild rose
Kansas: Sunflower
Kentucky: Goldenrod
Louisiana: Southern magnolia
Maine: Pine cone and tassel
Maryland: Black-eyed Susan
Massachusetts: Mayflower
Michigan: Apple blossom
Minnesota: Showy lady's-slipper
Mississippi: Magnolia
Missouri: Hawthorn
Montana: Bitterroot
Nebraska: Goldenrod
Nevada: Sagebrush
New Hampshire: Purple lilac
New Jersey: Purple violet

New Mexico: Yucca
New York: Rose
North Carolina: Dogwood
North Dakota: Wild prairie
rose
Ohio: Scarlet carnation
Oklahoma: Mistletoe
Oregon: Oregon grape
Pennsylvania: Mountain laurel
Rhode Island: Violet
South Carolina: Yellow jasmine
South Dakota: Pasqueflower

Tennessee: Iris
Texas: Bluebonnet
Utah: Sego lily
Vermont: Red clover
Virginia: Flowering dogwood
Washington: Coast rhodo-
dendron
West Virginia: Rosebay
rhododendron
Wisconsin: Butterfly violet
Wyoming: Wyoming paint
brush

Index

Water lilies, 32, 38, 39, 54, 57
　aphids on, 66
　feeding, 57
　winter protection, 98
Watkins, John V., 115
Watsonia: planting, 13-14, 31, 71, 79
　varieties, 14
Weed killers, chemical, 40, 49, 58,
　65-66, 220-222
　pre-emergent, 221-222
Weigela, 46
Weiss, Freeman, 138
Wheeler, Mrs. Lewis B., Jr., 137
White garden, 79
Wild, Gilbert H., & Son, 116-118
Wilson, E. H., 140

Winter aconite, 168
Wisteria: pruning, 64-65
　root pruning, 16
　tree form, 65
Witch-hazel, 87

Zantedeschia (calla lily), 31, 71, 169
Zephyranthes (rain lily), 57, 64, 169
　planting, 13, 24, 38, 45, 54, 71, 79
Zingiber (ginger lily), 10, 24
Zinnias: as cut flowers, 225, 226
　gibbing, 223
　indoors, 77, 86
　mildew, 50, 66
Zoysia grass (*Zoysia matrella*), 33, 69,
　183, 186